Alice Loyd

Collapse-Able

Three handbooks for living now and later

CENTER FOR ECOZOIC STUDIES

Collapse-Able: Three Handbooks for Living Now and Later
© 2024 Alice Loyd

All right reserved

Collapse-Able: Three Handbooks for Living Now and Later © 2024 by Alice Loyd is licensed under CC BY-NC-ND 4.0. To view a copy of this license, visit https://creativecommons.org/licenses/by-nc-nd/4.0/

Center for Ecozoic Studies
2516 Winningham Road
Chapel Hill
North Carolina 27516

Cover art and illustrations by Theo Egan

Book and cover design by Carl Brune

Printed in the USA

ISBN 979-8-9913523-0-7

*To my grandchildren
and all grandchildren, everywhere*

Contents

INTRODUCTION
1

HANDBOOK ONE
Growing Spiritual Strength for Hard Times

7

HANDBOOK TWO
Deepening Our Connections with Other Humans and the Rest of Nature

47

HANDBOOK THREE
Acquiring Useful Knowledge

83

CONCLUSION
A Time for the Future Oriented

153

APPENDIX I: IMPORTANT BOOKS IN MY READING PATH
161

APPENDIX II: FORMING A MINI-VILLAGE
166

APPENDIX III: CAWST BIOSAND FILTER CONSTRUCTION MANUAL: CONSTRUCTION STAGES B, E, AND H
175

NOTES
185

Acknowledgments

Sometimes authors say in the acknowledgments, "I couldn't have done it without her, or him." I've wondered what kind of help would make that much difference. Now I know that the statement likely recognizes a range of support rather than a single type of contribution. At least that's what I'm saying when I apply that sentence to Laurie Cone. Without her skill as editor offering better language alternatives, as proofreader finding almost invisible errors of punctuation or spacing, as science mentor correcting lay understandings and terms, and as master of general knowledge and astute social observer—without these assets which she generously gave to the project—this particular book would never have come into being.

CES publishing advisor Paul Wright and technical writer Sue Tideman also carefully read and suggested vital changes to the manuscript; Jennie Ratcliffe guided me through the last stages of book creation; and Theo Egan and Carl Brune contributed their artistry and skill to help the manuscript finally become a book.

I must also thank friends who offered encouragement by reading early stages of the manuscript and praising it in their circles, and above all the members of my family, including my late mother, who never doubted that I had at least one book in me, and that it might be a good one.

I owe special thanks to Herman Greene for the editorial and writing experience he gave me during our years together at the Center for Ecozoic Studies, and for his interest in seeing that this book came to publication.

Who else? I'm grateful to my large community of environmental activists, in North Carolina and across the country, whose passion to preserve the order and wonder of the planet has challenged me to do my part. And, perhaps surprisingly, I want to thank an editor who declined to publish the book. Caylie Graham believed in the quality and the subject matter despite its lack of commercial potential, and her rejection letter placed my work in the class of some writers I deeply admire.

To all the plants and creatures who have been my friends and guides throughout my life, I say thank you. And if, despite all of this excellent support, there remain errors of fact or judgment, they are mine alone.

Introduction
A TIME FOR THE STRONG-HEARTED

The world is changing. Along with every other member of the Earth community, humans live now at the edge of the unknown. The next fifty years are not likely to look much like the previous fifty. If we can approach the coming uncertainties as if we were explorers, stepping out onto an unfamiliar landscape with open eyes and hearts, the changes will be less threatening. Perhaps as one way of life is ending, we will find opportunities which that way of life did not afford. I think accepting this possibility is more realistic as well as more practical than clinging to what has been.

The signals of danger for creatures who need clean air, water, and food are abundant, but for industrial systems the many forms of pollution and habitat destruction have been the "necessary" marks of success. The misfortune of modern life is that the success of the economy is a threat to our survival. As English environmental writer and thinker Edward Goldsmith explained succinctly four decades ago, "Economic growth . . . is biological and social contraction. *They are just different sides of the same coin.*"[1]

And the challenge of our particular period of modern life is that economic growth based on biological and social contraction is nearing its end point. As the resources the economy requires for growth disappear or become financially unobtainable, the system based on their exploitation will begin to fail. We are likely to face the loss of industrial-era amenities at the same time we are dealing with a damaged planet.

How will we manage either of these hardships, much less both? In such an unfamiliar situation, where do we turn for help? And, you may be wondering as you begin to read, what information can a handbook offer that will help a person navigate this passage?

I suggest we begin by considering that the ecosystem, though injured, continues to support life. Seasons still turn, seeds still sprout, and in my part of North America this year, the Brood XIX periodical cicadas came out of the earth exactly thirteen years after their kind was last seen, to hum and lay eggs and die, as they have ever done. Many elements of biological life persist, though fewer and weaker, and so may we.

How has the ecosystem managed this well in the face of destruction? The answer is the reason for these handbooks: Earth is a flexible, tough, buoyant, and strong web of life—and we are a part of Earth. As difficulties mount, we can be sure that the survival capacities Earth has bred in us will become manifest if we put them to use. Just as evolution has prepared the rest of the biosphere to manage challenges, it has produced in humans the capacities we will need as the dangers increase.

We have both the strengths and the vulnerabilities of the whole of nature. I'm not saying we are invulnerable, or that Earth is. The assaults may surpass ecosystem tolerance, and thus ours as well. But the time to wilt is not yet. This is the time to join with Earth to realize our native resilience.

In the three handbooks I'm introducing, I will maintain that our most useful capacities as times get rougher will be those the industrial economy has overlooked and ignored—our spiritual and social faculties, and the creative aspect of our minds. These undervalued and thus typically less developed powers that evolution has had the wisdom to give us will be needed in the new era. My hope for this writing is to strengthen these abilities so that we are collapse-able—so that we are prepared to deal with whatever circumstances come our way.

"There is more to you than meets the eye," said Gandalf to Frodo.

J.R.R. TOLKIEN[2]

The three handbooks that follow are my effort to help younger people manage the decline of a far-from-perfect way of life by using a wider lens, one that includes not only such experiences as a person of my age might offer, but also the perspective of non-industrial cultures from today and back throughout human history.

Handbook One
STRENGTHENING OUR SPIRITS

The industrial way of life began and has succeeded by exploiting the human spirit. We have been shaped to seek comfort and to close our eyes to the corollary suffering. Few of us escaped the segmentations, externalizations, repressions, and conformities that make us passive consumers and willing employees. Whatever ease we have obtained through modern progress likely has been gained at the cost of something more precious: our sensitivities.

To know I have a thorn in my foot is fairly straightforward. It hurts when I walk. To recognize that something is missing is not so easy. By adulthood I will have filled the empty spot with whatever substitutes I can find. I will have grown callouses around the absence. I may have forgotten that it exists.

To uncover the heart's stifled longings is work of the spirit, and to do this we don't have to go on retreat, or quit our jobs, or join a sangha or a church or a twelve-step group. We might do any of these as we discover our deeper needs, and it's better to have support in any undertaking. But there is no set program and no universal book of instruction. What is required is more personal and of a higher level of difficulty: we must pay attention.

We must open ourselves. We must develop the sense that we belong here, that we are connected to the whole of existence. We are not born and then stranded by the planet that bore us. We have roots—however you may name them—that bind each of us to everything else. When we attend to the subtle messages from within and from our surroundings, we are recovering some of the capacities that make us fully alive. We will be blooming, as we were meant to do from the moment of birth.

It is these life-affirming assurances that will carry us through adversity. If you've lived through a world-ending event earlier in your life, you may have found that level of anchorage. In Handbook One, I will talk about the anchors that have sustained me. We are inextricably tied into the flow of life in this universe, even if no human agent is present to demonstrate the connection. We need to find these roots now, in order to be ready for whatever comes.

Handbook Two
DEEPENING OUR CONNECTIONS

A human is meant to live in the company of other caring humans from birth until death. Just as the more-than-human Earth web is intricately interwoven with a role for each member—none more worthy than another—so also the human community must be if humans are to thrive. The emphasis on individuals that Western culture advocates is an aberration, an abnormality in the history of the race. For a child to be normal within the ancient pattern, it must be nurtured in a nest of human guardians and teachers, and for those adults to behave normally toward a child or toward each other, they must have had the same upbringing. The results of generations of more modern, "civilized" child rearing are not pretty. If we often don't feel safe among our fellow humans, this is one explanation.

But we can create safe alliances. Humans come with 40,000 years of aptitude for cooperation and caring. Several thousand years marked by societal distrust have not erased the tendency to draw toward each other, as every disaster proves. It will take re-training and then practice for most mature Westerners to bond enduringly with others in common cause, but this is exactly what we must intend and then accomplish if we are to manage the upheaval that may accompany the disintegration of both the economic and the natural environments. We will need each other more than ever, even as threats to social cohesion accumulate. The handbook on deepening our connections is meant to help with this aspect of adaptation.

Handbook Three
ACQUIRING USEFUL KNOWLEDGE

To people in the more comfortable classes of the Global North, the ending of industrial civilization may at first seem to be the most serious of our problems. To lose services we've been able to buy with the wages of our participation in the economic system is a cause for concern, since most of us don't know how to manage without them. Daily we access technologies we understand only well enough to press the right buttons or the proper pedals. We eat food we know little about, even if we can afford the label "organic." We turn on faucets from which water appears as if by magic. We depend on life-extending medications we could not replicate if the pharmacies were to close.

The third handbook aims to help people prepare for a world without either the services we're accustomed to having others perform for us, or a reliable internet where we watch YouTube videos to learn new skills. In the near future, I think most of us will need to take more responsibility for the day's ordinary survival tasks, and while we will benefit by exchanging services with each other, I think we'll lose the option to remain ignorant about how to meet basic bodily needs. Only in the affluent nations of the Global North have typical humans lost the knowledge to grow food, obtain water without expert assistance, and manage their own sanitation, for example. One of the attractions of the intentional community where I chose to live is the nearby folk school,[3] where old skills are taught by practitioners committed to their preservation.

This part of adaptation will be a hard adjustment in developed nations, with most people facing it with fear and resistance. Speaking as an octogenarian raised in the Great Depression and World War II, I have to say I've been puzzled at the attitude toward work considered menial that I've found in many of my same-age peers. It is as if the post-war 1950s advertisements, with their glamorous depictions of labor-saving devices and chemicals, caused two generations of Americans to aim to rise above the duties that accompany being a human animal. Instead they were glad to put on Sunday clothes every day to go to the office, or leave home to operate or repair machinery in a shop, factory, or farm. They preferred to "get a job" so they could pay someone else to attend to anything regarded as lowly.

That stance is appropriate for people with serious physical limitations, but for able-bodied, mentally competent adults to disdain the ordinary work done past and present by most of the humans on the planet falls into some category of pretentiousness. Still, I don't want to minimize the difficulty of the shifts we can anticipate. People who are not well, not well-off financially, or not young enough or old enough to handle the labor involved have reason to fear the disappearance of institutions and services that have made their lives more comfortable. Pain and distress will increase according to a person's spiritual, social, and physical difficulties. The weak and sick will need the care of stronger companions to manage such a transition, and everyone needs a village of helping partners. But most readers who take the time to learn some new but very old skills can find satisfaction in creating a fairly graceful life even amid upheaval and difficulty. "Acquire useful knowledge now" is the advice I hope to persuade people to follow. Or as the Scouts say, "Be prepared."

My understanding of the preparation needed for the unpredictable but certainly less orderly period we are entering is based on experience, observation, and research. I know from experience that a quiet connection with sources of inner strength is the greatest comfort in times of trouble. From experience and observation I've learned that belonging to a respectful community is the best emotional as well as economic insurance we can provide for ourselves and our loved ones. From experience and research I've concluded that people who are secure spiritually and socially can learn how to manage the physical tasks of human daily life if they are physically able to perform them. To the extent they cannot—and at my age I must be included in that group—I have confidence that our spiritual and social strengths will stay with us as long as life lasts.

HANDBOOK ONE

Growing Spiritual Strength for Hard Times

Handbook One
GROWING SPIRITUAL STRENGTH FOR HARD TIMES

Contents

STRONG SPIRITS, NOURISHED BY THE GOODNESS OF THE COSMOS, WILL CARRY US THROUGH ADVERSITY / 10

    A spiritual path begins wherever we are / 11

    For me the path has been led by the eternal verities / 13

WE CAN REGULARLY GIVE GOODNESS OUR FULL ATTENTION / 15

    We can respond from the heart / 15

    We can give attention to goodness in regular practice / 17
        PRACTICE OPENING THE HEART / 18
        PRACTICE CHOOSING THE GOOD / 20

    We can give attention to the ultimate mysteries / 22
        DEATH / 22; LOVE / 23; GOD / 23; EVIL / 24; MIRACLES / 25; NATURE / 26

WE CAN SPEND TIME WITH PEOPLE WHO EXEMPLIFY GOODNESS / 28

        KINDNESS / 28; INTEGRITY / 28; LOYALTY / 28; LOVING SACRIFICE / 29; JUSTICE / 29; FORGIVENESS / 30

WE CAN BE INSPIRED BY WRITINGS THAT ILLUMINATE GOODNESS / 30

        SEEKING TRUTH IN NON-FICTION / 30
        SEEING VIRTUE IN FICTION / 32

WE CAN DEMONSTRATE GOODNESS IN OUR OWN BEHAVIOR / 33

    Exercising the agency of fairness / 33
        RECOGNIZING UNFAIR ADVANTAGE / 34
        QUESTIONING CONSUMER BEHAVIOR / 35
        WITHDRAWING SUPPORT FROM AN UNFAIR SYSTEM / 35
        RELEASING ATTACHMENT TO BENEFITS / 36

    Exercising the agency of truth / 37
        TRUTH-SEEKING IN PERSONAL HISTORY / 38
        TRUTH-TELLING IN PUBLIC ADVOCACY / 38
        FINE POINTS OF TRUTH-SEEKING AND TRUTH-TELLING / 41

IN CONCLUSION / 42

STRONG SPIRITS, NOURISHED BY THE GOODNESS OF THE COSMOS, WILL CARRY US THROUGH ADVERSITY

"I'm ready for whatever happens." The people who see the difficulties ahead and yet feel this well-prepared may not be the ones with a year's supply of food in metal cans or a shelf full of efficiently-rotated bottles of water. The old man who sits by the window in his wheelchair may live with that serenity, or the tired nurse, rushing each day to catch the morning bus. They can face hardship without living in fear because they have spiritual strength, which is an internal possession. A strong-hearted person with deep inner resources is ready to deal with either prosperity or adversity. For that person, a collapse in the exterior world would be disturbing, but it would not be an insurmountable event.

It is helpful to have external support when we seek to build internal strength, but by definition a spiritual quest takes place within. Although influenced by outer events and outside actors, the spiritual life is an inner event. I can be inspired—inspirited—by what others do and say, but I am the one who allows inspiration to take place. Through my own spirit, I can connect with the deepest elements of life on Earth.

For we are not alone, living on the side of an indifferent planet whirling through space. Earth holds us all at her breast—every creature, every geological feature. It is my belief that food for the spirit comes from the same source as food for the body—from this planet in this universe. Here is where we are. There is nowhere else to be. All we need of nourishment, physically or spiritually, is to be found in this place.

> *If you put your soul against this oar with me,*
> *the power that made the universe will enter your sinew*
> *from a source not outside your limbs, but from a holy realm*
> *that lives in us.*[4]

So spoke the Persian poet Rumi, thirteenth-century Islamic scholar and Sufi mystic. All of the resources of an endlessly creative capacity are here to sustain us. Our society has not encouraged us to explore the intangible features either of ourselves or of nature, partly because prevailing philosophy has maintained they don't exist, since they can't be quantified. Their existence is an internal phenomenon to be observed only by the one who experiences them.

As a result of this atmosphere of denial, our spirits may be underdeveloped. To strengthen them, we must enter their realm and explore it for ourselves. When we do, our spiritual leanings will remain superficial if we merely accept the ideas others have offered. If your path can be labeled, it's probably someone else's, not your own. Someone else's path is fine as a starting place. From there you can find out for yourself the implications of that teaching.

> I shall speak of nothing of which I have no experience, either in my own life or in observation of others, or which the Lord has not taught me in prayer.[5]

St. Teresa of Avila, the great Spanish mystic and reformer, wrote those words almost four centuries ago. I am encouraging you to do as she did: explore your spirit's capacities for yourself. To the extent you do, your spiritual orientation will not be merely intellectual assent; it will arise from your unique journey. No matter where you start, if you continue to follow your heart, you may find yourself outside the boundaries of the tradition in which you began.

A spiritual path begins wherever we are

> *If you are searching*
> *You must not stop until you find.*
> *When you find, however,*
> *You will be troubled.*
> *Your confusion will give way to wonder.*
> *In wonder you will reign over all things.*
>
> GOSPEL OF THOMAS[6]

First, then, comes the searching, the sincere desire to find the roots from which we came and by which we can stay afloat—even reign—over confusion and turmoil. And though what our spirits desire is found within and speaks with a silent voice, it is not small. Rather, in Rumi's words, it is the power that made the universe. It will enter our sinews, give us passion for the quest, and lead us into a state of wonder.

Where we begin is up to each of us, but I began with what I knew of the life and teachings of Jesus. I grew up reading the King James Bible, resonating with the texts that spoke about justice and love while ignoring the parts that violated my sense of right—as with other literature. It has always seemed to me the early judgments I made about biblical texts or the opinions of grownups around me were guided by assumptions with which I was born. At least it is clear to me that by the age of eight or nine I had come to my own conclusions about a number of serious matters. I remember hearing a sermon that denounced a period of Israelite history when "every man did that which was right in his own eyes" (Judg. 21:25 KJV). As a child in the pew, I disagreed with the preacher's view that this was a bad thing.

At around this same age I had a realization that has become the foundation of my spiritual life. Unrelated to anything happening around me, one day I suddenly understood that fairness was something that didn't have to be seen to be real. I saw with certainty that while I might not be treated fairly myself, fairness was a real thing that could not be destroyed. As a mistreated child, I embraced this assurance, and I hate to think how bleak my life would have felt without it. Through that one insight—that fairness is firmly in place despite appearances to the contrary—I gained certainty that the world is good and that its goodness will endure, no matter what. To express the feeling that realization gave me then and continues to give, I turn to a moment in *Lord of the Rings* when Samwise the hobbit finds reassurance:

> *There, peeping among a cloud-wrack, above a dark tor high up in the mountains, Sam saw a white star twinkle for a while. The beauty of it smote his heart as he looked up out of the forsaken land, and hope returned to him. For, like a shaft clear and cold, the thought pierced him that in the end the Shadow was only a small and passing thing: there was light and high beauty forever beyond its reach. . . . He crawled back into the brambles and laid himself by Frodo's side, and putting away all fear he cast himself into a deep, untroubled sleep.*[7]

The star was a sign of goodness enduring beyond the reach of evil. To Sam it meant that good was working in the world even when evil appeared triumphant, as it seemed to be in that hostile terrain he and Frodo were struggling to cross. The knowledge gave him peace, although nothing else in his situation had changed. So it was for me, when I understood the unalterable existence of fairness as spiritual reality.

For me the path has been led by the eternal verities

Transcendent ideals such as truth, beauty, and fairness—which can also be called justice—are real, and they are present even when lies, ugliness, and injustice seem to prevail. Regardless of whether they are applied in the world around us, these values exist and we can take heart from them.

Wendell Berry writes,

> *Among the necessary and the least dispensable words in our language are those by which we name our values. Here is a list (surely not complete) of such words: Truth, Mercy, Justice, Forgiveness, Peace, Equality, Trust, Hospitality, Generosity, Freedom, Love, Neighborliness, Home, Reverence, Beauty, Care, Courtesy, Goodness, Faith, Kindness, Health, Wholeness, Holiness. It is obvious, first of all, how unhappily these words and the thoughts they name must associate with the materialism, the several determinisms, ideal of mechanical efficiency, and the rule of profit and war, which now intrude so powerfully into their company. . . .*
>
> *The great general principles are like an old tree's trunk and main branches that sway but do not break.*[8]

These words and the positive values they stand for exist unavoidably alongside other values: materialism that puts things above life; determinisms that say our actions are beyond our ability to control; the idealization of efficiency and machines; and the rule of profit and war. The beneficial ideals get trampled by opposing standards every day, but the values the words name are not destroyed by the world's winds.

In a workshop I attended in 2009, Buddhist scholar and social activist Joanna Macy asked attendees to name a feature of Earth life under threat that we felt especially sad about losing. Among the many answers I heard—certain animals going extinct, beloved rivers polluted, glaciers melting—someone said, "Truth." Macy let it go by, but I wanted to protest. Truth is not under threat. It cannot be lost. People may lie, but they are not destroying truth. I may not know what is true in some cases, and I might destroy my own character in an effort to make a lie appear true, but truth exists beyond all possible harm. It is like an old tree's trunk and main branches that sway but do not break.

The first name I learned for these spiritual values is "eternal verities,"[9] which *Oxford Learner's Dictionary* calls "fundamental and inevitably true values." Because they are good, I also call them virtues. These virtues are not creations of someone's mind. They aren't wishful thinking. We recognize them using our internal faculties, but they exist whether we realize them or not. And for me, the category of goodness is an umbrella under which all the other virtues reside. We call each of these "good": truth, fairness, kindness, beauty, courtesy, holiness, loyalty, fidelity, generosity. To demonstrate one of these qualities is a good thing to do.

Mystic, author, and teacher Cynthia Bourgeault calls them nutrients, and she says they bring strength into the human for the benefit of the world.

> *These are nutrients to our being and nutrients to the world. We have the capacity to transform them, to produce them and to put them in the atmosphere of this planet, and one would say we not only have the capacity to do that but we have the responsibility.*[10]

They are agents for good, spiritual ingredients that the one who receives them is to share. When Jesus said to his followers, "I have meat to eat that ye know not of (John 4:32 KJV)," I think he was talking about this kind of nourishment.

For me they are values that show us what is right and good, despite what the culture may be saying. However you may refer to them—values, nutrients, virtues, eternal verities, or transcendent ideals—they feed the heart and give direction. As I look back on my life I see how strongly they have directed me from eight years old until today. Though I have forgotten, slipped, and failed at times to follow their wisdom, they have remained constant. I believe they nourish humans because they emerge from the goodness of the cosmos, as we do. I see four means by which we can invite them to bring strength to our spirits:

(1) We can regularly give them our full attention.

(2) We can spend time with people who exemplify them.

(3) We can be inspired by writings that illuminate them.

(4) We can try to demonstrate them in our own behavior.

These practices have been an important part of my own spiritual journey. I will devote a section of this handbook to each practice.

WE CAN REGULARLY GIVE GOODNESS OUR FULL ATTENTION

My connection to the planet is greater than gravity. I have roots that go down deep into the soul of Earth, just as everything else does. Nothing on Earth is unconnected to this core. This is what life is, and the connection is what makes life good. The things that recognize and honor the connection are good things. Whatever does not honor what I am trying to name here is not good.

Some good things are physical, concrete. You can see them walking, standing, waving in the breeze. Those come and go. But some good things are only visible to the inner eye, and these do not change. They are the things we call spiritual.

I am sure that for many people it is not as easy to embrace unseen qualities with their hearts as it would be to connect with a person who evokes them. Whether a person, a set of words, or any other signal beckons us into the spiritual aspect of ourselves and of the world, however, at that point our experience is unique. What I offer is my own path inward, to the place where I am connected at a deeper level, where I am never alone.

We can respond from the heart

The reader may notice that I make a distinction between spiritual and religious. In this handbook my subject is not religion, although I use religious texts. Neither am I speaking of beliefs. Spiritual wisdom comes through the heart. The heart is our link with the whole circle of being, and only what affirms the welfare of the whole circle can nourish our spirits. Whatever is heartless, uncaring, or indifferent to the good of all is in opposition to our roots and reduces spiritual strength.

History tells us that religious people have committed many acts of cruelty and oppression while calling their actions good. I marvel more every day, in fact, that my unique path began with the focus on fairness, a concern that has forever tied me to the welfare of the whole community. Humans are interlinked with each other and with nature; we are designed to care, to protect, and to serve living beings in physical ways on this physical planet. Confront almost any human with an urgent and personal need and that person will respond with helpfulness.

But the impulse to help can be checked by fear—"I might get hurt." It can also be checked by doctrine, policy, rule, dogma or principle. Religious dogma that considers non-adherents less worthy of respect than believers does not support practices that benefit all of life. The record shows the damage such beliefs can generate. As a child, I recognized that some instruction I found in the Bible could not be considered good, since it called for doing great harm. Distinguishing between what is good and what is not good in religious teachings is as important as determining what is good or not good in the world around us. This is spiritual work each of us must undertake, and I am fortunate to have begun it early, and under the guidance of the principle of fairness.

When we recognize that something is good, whether in religious teachings or daily life, the spiritual response is deeper than intellectual assent. I'm sure a person can set out to do a good thing for reasons other than heartfelt caring. The spiritual life, however, is not an attempt to achieve some degree of perfection or innocence. Mistakes are allowed. Spiritual insight is an embrace. When we recognize goodness, the spiritual response is to embrace it from the heart.

We all have help as we determine what is good. When he was twelve years old, Thomas Berry had an experience that answered the question for him.

> *It was an early afternoon in May when I first looked down over the scene and saw the meadow. The field was covered with lilies rising above the thick grass. A magic moment, this experience gave to my life something, I know not what, that seems to explain my life at a more profound level than almost any other experience I can remember.*
>
> *This early experience, it seems, has become normative for me throughout the range of my thinking. Whatever preserves and enhances this meadow in the natural cycles of its transformation is good; what is opposed to this meadow or negates it is not good. My life orientation is that simple.*[11]

Berry oriented his life around protecting the lilies, the field, and all growing, living things—not out of a detached, impersonal belief that it was the right thing to do, but because this beautiful field and all it represented was in his eyes endearing. His heart went out to it.

In *A Sand County Almanac*, Aldo Leopold offers the same standard of goodness: "A thing is right when it tends to preserve the integrity, stability and beauty of the biotic community. It is wrong when it tends otherwise."[12] The widely read book that contains this definition shows Leopold's ardent embrace of it.

His measurement of good and bad doesn't answer all questions, of course. What might help one part of the biotic community might hurt another, and I lack the knowledge to know always how my actions might affect the entirety. Now we see as "through a glass, darkly" (1 Cor. 13:12 KJV) regarding ecological wisdom, but in most cases we know toward which direction an act "tends," to use Leopold's term.

I believe my heart wanted the meadow and the biotic community to do well long before I was old enough for my mind to grasp the reality of an unseen principle such as fairness. I was open to the goodness of the visible world and also to the goodness of less visible realms.

The fact that my perception of fairness at the age of eight has changed as I've learned more about the concept doesn't mean there is no constant ideal. It is not fairness that has altered, but my understanding of it, which, if I am sincere as I consider it, will continue to grow. Deepening my comprehension of what a concept means when applied in particular situations is in fact the only way I can continue to value it. I must ask, "What is fairness in this case?" I must question assumptions, looking for culturally implanted ideas that may differ from the ideal. Throughout my life, though, I can have faith that fairness exists, as I realized in early years.

We can give attention to goodness in regular practice

I've been asked why I speak of the verities as spiritual guides and not simply enduring ethical principles. One difference lies in the way I relate to these values. I open my heart to them. I experience them as bound up with the character of the universe, which to me is sacred. They have magnetic appeal, and I respond with my emotions as well as my moral sense. Certainly a person could practice truthfulness or fairness without being stirred into reverence, but what I'm naming here is my own response.

Cynthia Bourgeault sees a deeper reason.

These things are not just nice character traits; they're actual subtle energetic nutrients. And we human beings are charged with producing them out of the fruit of our own transformed life. When we don't, there's a deterioration in the environment, which is not only a deterioration in the mental and emotional environment but in the actual physiology and overall energetic balance of the planet.[13]

I once read a story about an elderly woman in a nursing home. She sat in a wheelchair in her room or in the hallway day after day, without visitors or hope of regaining health, yet she was always cheerful when people came by and spoke. One day an attendant asked how she managed the long hours alone. "Oh, it's not hard," she answered. "I think about God."

As she thought about God, I believe she was making changes in the overall energetic balance of the planet. Everything about this story indicates that despite her limitations, this woman was acting as a power for good. A verse I underlined in my Bible during my teen years called me to do the same:

Finally, brethren, whatsoever things are true, whatsoever things are honest, whatsoever things are just, whatsoever things are pure, whatsoever things are lovely, whatsoever things are of good report; if there be any virtue, and if there be any praise, think on these things (Phil. 4:8 KJV).

PRACTICE OPENING THE HEART

Sometimes I think on these things at bedtime or during wakeful hours at night. When I need a reset, I turn my thoughts toward the goodness that has always shown itself if I wait. Since that experience at eight years old, I don't think I've ever doubted the world is good—that is, the spiritual world that can't be shaken. And if I want to, I can feel again the bliss of that knowledge. I can dwell on the good fortune of being connected with the world's goodness, and as gratitude rushes in, I sense goodness all around me.

Or on another occasion truth might be my focus. I might examine my commitment to being truthful. As I unfold myself before the light of that virtue, I am chastened by my failures but heartened by its existence. How glad I am that there is a plumb line so firm, one that can't be distorted or seduced away. When my heart opens to my longing for a deeper bond with truth, I feel myself lining up with this value in a sensory way. The resonance is like a bell ringing.

> *Exuberance is existence, time a husk.*
> *When the moment cracks open, ecstasy leaps out and devours space.*
> *Love goes mad with the blessings, like my words give.*
>
> RUMI[14]

In my vision of reality, all that is good in the world of spirit exists somewhere down in the center of things—not up in the sky or far out beyond the universe. The connection I have with this goodness is from my heart. When I concentrate on the connection, I go through my heart to where all the good things gather, whatever you may call them: ideals, virtues, spirits, ancestors, angels, heaven. My focus on these ideals matches what others say about meditation practice: it makes me happy. I rest in emotional and spiritual wonder, an experience that has been shown to activate our bodies' healing hormones, while turning off the hormones related to stress.

Outward symbols are another path inward. For me, J.R.R. Tolkien's descriptions of elves in *Lord of the Rings* paint a glowing picture of goodness. According to biographer John Garth, goodness is what Tolkien meant the elves to represent.[15] In one scene the hobbits Frodo and Bilbo are in the Elfdom of Rivendell, reunited there after Frodo was attacked by the Black Riders.

> In spite of his delight in Bilbo's company Frodo felt a tug of regret as they passed out of the Hall of Fire. Even as they stepped over the threshold a single clear voice rose in song. Frodo halted for a moment, looking back. ... He stood still enchanted, while the sweet syllables of the elvish song fell like clear jewels of blended word and melody. . . . "They will sing that, and other songs of the Blessed Realm, many times tonight," said Bilbo.
>
> They spoke no more of the small news of the Shire far away, nor of the dark shadows and perils that encompassed them, but of the fair things they had seen in the world together, of the Elves, of the stars, of trees, and the gentle fall of the bright year in the woods.[16]

When I'm in the blessed realm of the inner life, I begin to feel less anxious. After a while my guard may fall away so that I see my enemies in a new light. Recently in one of those times a certain person came to mind and I suddenly thought, "I'll go and thank him for doing that!" He had made a generous contribution when we took a collection. In that moment I saw his gift as a sign that what he believes about himself—that he is good, that he has the good of others in mind—I saw that, in some way, what he believes might be true. In that flash I had a glimpse of his heart, and I felt I could talk with him later from that insight.

Another statement from St. Teresa of Avila reveals the practice that would make that generous perspective more likely.

> I have a lovely habit.
> At night in my prayers, I touch everyone I have seen that day.
> I shape my heart like theirs and theirs like mine.
>
> ST. TERESA OF AVILA[17]

I'm drawn to that practice. I don't always live from this place of generosity, but I'm glad to know I can move in that direction again and again. In such moments, I can believe with my heart as well as my mind that everyone belongs in the blessed realm, even when they work to oppose its values. I know that sometimes people who are hurting others believe they are doing good. Those people are deceived, and in order to fully serve goodness they must undertake the work of becoming undeceived.

PRACTICE CHOOSING THE GOOD

Of course, I also recognize that humans have the capacity to choose to do harm for harm's sake. No one is compelled to live in accord with the values of the universe. But though history or genes may shape a child's growing character toward hurting others, once we become adults we're each free, at some level, to choose whether to love life or hate it, whether to flourish on the soul plane or to sicken.

There is the story of the two wolves. An old man said to his grandson, "A fight between two wolves is going on inside me. One wolf is evil: anger, envy, greed, arrogance, self-pity, and resentment. The other wolf is good: peace, love, humility, kindness, generosity, and compassion. The same fight is going on inside you, grandson, and inside everyone."

The boy was silent for a minute and then asked, "Which wolf will win?"

The old man answered, "The one you feed."

As the story asserts, at any time any one of us may feed the wolf that is evil. Inadvertently or knowingly, we may choose to do what is harmful. There is always a helpful course of action, however, and our role is to discern what it is. My commitment to the verities requires me to distinguish between good and bad with increasing accuracy and to invest my time and energy toward what Buddhists call Right Action.

> Right Action is a part of the Noble Eightfold Path taught by the Buddha. It includes, first of all, the kinds of actions that can help humans and other living beings who are being destroyed by war, political oppression, social injustice, and hunger. To protect life, prevent war, and serve living beings, we need to cultivate our energy of lovingkindness.
>
> THICH NHAT HANH[18]

Behavior that is clearly harmful may reflect the evolution of our species. Some research supports the view that brain development explains why some humans operate more from fear than others do, and fear is at the base of most hostility and, I suppose, of greed as well. But it is undeniable that our culture fosters alienation, distrust, and fear-based self-interest. We are not encouraged to connect with the positive values that give strength to our hearts. The most prominent voices deliberately stir up fear as a means to increase their own power or wealth.

I have an obligation to turn away from harmful influences and turn toward the constructive ideals embraced by a few in every generation. And whenever I feed the good that lives inside me, I become a positive influence. The whole web benefits with every recognition I give to these values. Older, Indigenous cultures teach that it is our duty to give spiritual support to the functions of nature. Like the Navajo boy who runs to help the sun run his daily journey, when I allow the virtues to strengthen me, I am also strengthening their power throughout the world.

Although individualistic religion focuses on personal salvation, a spiritual practice is not primarily for the benefit of the seeker. Science is now demonstrating what mystics have always told us: our spirits as well as our bodies are interwoven with the one web of being. I think we benefit from all the prayers that have ever been prayed that are true to the character of our universe. That means our own moments of reverence will radiate throughout the wide inner dimension.

We can give attention to the ultimate mysteries

Up to this point I haven't discussed death, love, God, evil, miracles, or nature to any extent, although these subjects are all relevant to the strengthening of our spirits. With humility I will give here a few tentative views, although I suspect any plain countrywoman of pre-Roman times in the British Isles of my ancestry could have shared far richer insights. My upbringing in the impoverished spirituality of Protestantism, Western science, and modern medicine shed little light on these mysteries, and after years of considering I still have many questions.

DEATH

I believe spirit is an aspect of all physical existence. It is common to expect the spiritual part of us to live on after death, and my experience suggests it is true. The most concrete example in my life took place when my eighteen-year-old companion cat died. On the next night, he came through my bedside window, landed on the other side of the bed with a thump I could feel, and jumped onto my chest where my arms went around his tangible body for an instant before he lifted off and vanished. A moment of tenderness, and he was gone. This was not something I had ever imagined possible, but when I told a cat-loving friend, she said, "After Buddy died, that night I felt him jump onto our bed, and my partner felt it too."

One way we might explain the event in the light of modern science is to view spirit as the unseen alternate capacity of matter. Quantum physics has taught us about the ephemeral nature of sub-atomic physical properties: particle transforms into wave, matter becomes energy, in alternate but unified existence. It seems to me these findings suggest how we might come into matter at birth and in death return into energy.

I do think there is an eternal aspect to matter, that its demise on our plane means some kind of emergence on another. My spiritual path has led me to experience this other field of existence, the place where all spiritual values and entities reside, and this will surely be there for me after my death as it is now. I don't have much curiosity about the details, however. I may, like the supernova, burst into transformation beyond recognition. To have lived in the Earth realm has been a gift I will release gladly. By the time of my death, I hope I'll have given away every asset, physical and spiritual. All the love, joy, and peace I've known in this life I aim to disperse as abundantly as they have been given. If I'm true to my aspiration, of course, these spiritual gifts will grow and rebound. They are the magic penny that increases the more it is spent.

LOVE

There is consensus among people who care about such things that love is the primary spiritual value, the ultimate good. If defined as benign attachment, then love is what holds everything together.

All of the positive ideals help to define the quality we call love, for they promote well-being, and whatever promotes well-being is acting in the way love acts. The epicenter from which they spring is the kind of love visible in the creative, life-giving physical universe. This is not the romantic sentiment of popular music, but the impartially generous love we see in those who serve the needs of a family, a community, or a world. It is *agape*: love without regard to self-benefit.

In spirit or in physical form, this love is always in relationship. When I was drawn as a child into the sphere of the ideal of fairness, the experience felt personal. I responded to it with my whole heart, as I would to an embrace. I think moving into the realm of spirit always feels that way, because the nature of spirit is love.

GOD

That is why, in searching for an understanding of the concept of God, we sometimes say "God is love" (I John 4:8 KJV). The other verities on Wendell Berry's list of ideals are also godly attributes, and when I fully open to their presence, my perception is that I am open to God, or the Source, or the Center, or the One. By applying any name, however — making God a noun — I don't mean to say God is a fixed substance, an omnipotent cosmic individual.

The ancient Hebrews named God as I Am, the principle of Being. Alfred North Whitehead sees God as the creativity within and around all the becoming that has occurred from the beginning.[19] It is as if the entire macrocosm, both manifested and unmanifested, exists in or alongside a creative presence, and yet there is no outside or inside. The mystery at the core of existence is beyond my mind to understand, but yet as close as my heart. I like these words by theologian David Bentley Hart: "The question of God never ceases to pose itself anew, and the longing to know about God never wholly abates."[20]

EVIL

Earth residents face destructive winds, deadly fires, and raging waters. They get injured and sick. This is planetary reality, the results of the properties that belong to the elements of nature. But while destruction as well as creation is a feature of evolutionary order, this order does not act with malice toward any life form. Just as all receive impartially the benefits of life on the planet, so also do all engage with the risks.

Lightning doesn't strike a tree or a man in a display of domination. The lion doesn't feed upon the lamb to show its power. In the Earth economy, for one creature to live at all requires taking or altering the life of another. It is a life-supportive arrangement, not an evil. The only malevolent actions that will be directed toward particular life forms or groups will come from human beings.

It is the human power of choice that allows life-destroying, spirit-quenching behavior. This evolutionary development came with peril: since we can choose how to behave, we can do damage as well as good. In other words, evil is not embedded in the cosmos in the way good is. It is rather an interruption of natural order by a human agent. It is the absence of goodness on a particular occasion, a failure to align with life on the part of individuals or groups of individuals.

To follow the Leopold definition that I quoted earlier, a thing is wrong, or evil, when it tends to disrupt the integrity, stability and beauty of the biotic community. Cultures that uphold values supportive of community establish procedures by which cohesion is maintained, and as a result they have fewer deviant members. Unfortunately, in the societies that now dominate the globe these values have been violated rather than upheld for centuries, with increasingly apparent consequences. The empire of global capital in which we are now enmeshed is disrupting the biotic community—including humans—to a degree no mind can fully grasp, generating chaos and suffering and high levels of violence.

And while at this time the whole world is being wronged and life itself is being attacked by powerful actors, the beneficial order is still in place. It lives and grows in the hearts of humans who love it, and other species delight in it by their very nature. If the elaborate, awe-inspiring brilliance of Cenozoic-era Earth should be dismantled, even its physical manifestation will continue in some now-unimaginable fashion. We can be sure that its essential goodness will remain intact.

MIRACLES

At first I called this section "supernatural occurrences," because as the writer David Abram once said, our culture views as supernatural anything that can't be duplicated in a laboratory. I've already mentioned some experiences that seem beyond everyday explanation. My entire life story, in fact, can be seen as a miraculous delivery from harm— or at times into a harm that brought with it good that I wouldn't have obtained in any other way, given my limitations. Indeed, since we are all so bound together in this web of mind, feeling, and action, chains of events and coincidences that appear miraculous can hardly be avoided.

But more spectacular occurrences may require another explanation: faith healing, bilocation (being in two places at once), and communication with the dead, for example. Since such phenomena are often the claims of charlatans and money-making schemes, it is tempting to doubt reports and wise to question. I still offer a cautious yes to such possibilities.

The thinness of physical-spiritual boundaries has been demonstrated by wisdom masters, Jesus being the one I know most about. He healed the sick and taught his disciples to do the same in his name, which means by the principle he practiced, which was love. Shamanic medicine has been shown effective in traditional cultures, and energy healing is not unknown in our midst. Placebo experiments show that faith is a powerful spiritual influence. I try to remain open to anything that promotes the general good.

I sometimes have moments of the focused quality of faith that might accomplish something out of the ordinary—if I could hold to that focus. In my mental imagery at these times is a channel which I have entered. The "I" in that channel, for that fragment of time, is pure self without awareness of my frailty. But that moment tends to be cut short by fear that keeps me from walking on water. I falter as Peter did when fear overcame his faith, when he walked for a moment toward Jesus on the surface of the lake.[21]

I think people with less fear and more durable attention within that narrow channel might certainly accomplish what would be called miracles, particularly if an intention is shared by a number of people.

One explanation might lie in the energy-alternating-with-mass theory I've already mentioned. Quantum physics documents both bilocation and the influential role of the observer in the behavior of subatomic particles. Whether in subatomic realms or in larger beings, our separateness from each other and from spirit is a misconception.

When the person I'm thinking of calls me on the phone, or I run into an acquaintance from England when I'm visiting Philadelphia, I think either our bondedness or the quantum explanation may be responsible. Whatever the underlying mechanism, these are glimpses into the deeper workings of the universe. In the amazing world we live in, we should not be surprised when we sometimes encounter the unexplainable, at least by current knowledge. Encounters rare in Western culture but frequent in other parts of the world are recorded by writers I credit in the reading list in Appendix I. As we seek the "integrity, stability and beauty of the biotic community," and open ourselves to the internal as well as the external aspects of this orientation, I think we will find much beyond current, everyday Western understandings.

NATURE

No currently prevailing beliefs of the dominant culture are more likely to be overturned than those regarding the natural world. Our language fails us as tragically when speaking of the oneness of humans with the rest of nature as it does with the oneness of body and spirit. There are not two realities. There is one—the physical-spiritual-mental-emotional world—and this entire discussion of death, love, evil, God, and miracles is as true for the rest of nature as it is for the humans who can read the words.

Plants too have spiritual as well as physical properties, as do elephants, mosquitos, clouds, and the sun. We live amid enchantment, and as far as we know, only finite, free-to-choose-good-or-evil *Homo sapiens* has become unable to see the world whole. For most people, though, an experience in nature can evoke a degree of pleasure that moves easily into reverence, and this is the reason: our bodies long to experience unity with our relative species—who have never lost sight of the unity. They will extend welcome whenever we move toward them with the proper respect.

I feel, however, the truth of Andreas Weber's caution against a superficial view of nature's functions.

> Nature is neither the safe haven in which to take shelter from the ailments of civilization nor the perfect model for a healthier existence. Many idyllic views of nature . . . anthropomorphize nature and forget that its power is not a mirror of our emotions but a deep interpenetration of creative and imaginative forces, which can be destructive as well as benign. . . . These deep principles cannot be verbalized, as this would disentangle them from their interwovenness.[22]

Nature isn't "pretty" or "nice." As with other realities too large for our minds to grasp, the appropriate response is wonder and gratitude. The images from the James Webb Space Telescope are a call to a proper respect. To see hundreds of galaxies, each containing a hundred million stars and some so distant they go back almost to the beginning—the only response is awe, without comment or explanation.

In an older culture my tribe would not have left appreciation of these mysteries to chance. From childhood I would have been part of conversations that placed me firmly within the tribe's acquired store of wisdom. At the edge of adulthood I might have been given explicit words of guidance and then taken to a lonely setting where I would stay, until through fasting and dreaming I would find my role in the universe, so that I could take my place among the group's adults. In an even older culture, the posture might have been so explicit through living moment to moment from Earth's almost literally apparent breast, that no guidance was needed. For indeed there are no words adequate to describe the depth of our dependency and gratitude. Only dance and song come close. Religions arise from the attempt.

The economic and cultural setting in which we now live has made it hard to find enough nourishment for our spirits to thrive. The public spirituality, as Thomas Berry writes, lacks "any significant evaluation of the larger context of our lives. On both sides, the scientific and the religious, there is a naïveté that is ruinous to the human community, to the essential functioning of the biosphere, and eventually to the Earth itself."[23] No generation has ever before encountered the physical dangers with which we are confronted so ill equipped to deal with them. Each of us must find a way within ourselves. The eternal verities are the guides I've followed, and they have never failed me.

WE CAN SPEND TIME WITH PEOPLE WHO EXEMPLIFY GOODNESS

KINDNESS

The virtues are the lights I followed, and what I needed after discovering them was humans to show me the full measure of their value. There have been many. One who appeared at a crucial moment was Mrs. LaFoy, a teacher who tapped me on the shoulder in the halls of my junior high school and said in a friendly voice, "I've been watching you, and I have an idea." Out of my enduring gratitude, many years later I followed up on an impulse, found her phone number through Information, and made the call. "Of course I remember you!" that voice assured me once more—she in her mid-eighties by then but still full of friendly warmth. The eternal ideal of kindness exists, and there are people whose lives make it visible.

INTEGRITY

We need to know people who demonstrate the beneficial values, and when we find them we must respond. At fourteen when Mrs. LaFoy called me aside and invited me to try for an honor that seemed far above me, I said yes, although at the time I was discouraged and filled with shame. On other occasions I've been the one to reach out, as when I overheard a woman asking important questions of an official in a comfortable manner as we all rode an elevator at the State Office Building. When we both exited near the door of the cafeteria, I turned to her and asked if she'd like to have lunch with me. The outcome was a lasting friendship with a Quaker who, by living from well-thought-out egalitarian, peace-affirming positions, has exemplified a virtue I haven't yet mentioned, integrity. There is such a thing as integrity, although it seems more rare these days, especially in public figures. She has shown me how the ideal looks in practice—to be whole and undivided, with actions consistent with principles.

LOYALTY

Other virtues have come alive for me through my friends. One friend illustrates for me the ideal of loyalty. With her well-ordered life and wise choices, I often marveled that she could see the complications in mine and yet remain close. She was there when I had to call on someone, and her faith in me gave me faith in myself. Through many years and long distances our bond has stayed strong because she stays strong in her commitment, responding to every change of our interests and fortunes with the same openheartedness and respect.

LOVING SACRIFICE

Through another friend I came to understand loving sacrifice—the appropriate giving of one's best effort in spite of the cost. When her son, who had a wife in a wheelchair and a daughter to raise, began to have symptoms of amyotrophic lateral sclerosis (ALS), this woman—herself needing hip repair—took on the role of nurse and housekeeper and did it gracefully. As her son's disease advanced, she mastered the technical tasks of his medical regimen and made it possible for him to remain in charge of his life and treatment. When he went to a hospital in a different city, she moved nearby and continued her role, even before and after her own surgery and rehab, when she could barely walk.

JUSTICE

Another friend brings into sharp focus the first ideal I discovered. From her teens when her high school integrated, she has been a justice activist, and her commitment deepened when she was older and spent time in Africa. As a teacher helping to integrate an elementary school in the US South, as a social worker assisting with refugee resettlement—meeting weary, bewildered immigrants as they enter this country and connecting them with resources each would need to make a new life—she sought employment that directly expressed her belief in non-violent justice. In retirement in her 60s, she pursued a master's degree in conflict resolution, organized a project to teach non-violence to children, and studied issues of water protection to increase her effectiveness as a clean water advocate. She is a "Raging Granny" in every sense of the title, singing with a group under that name at rallies and traveling throughout the country even in her eighties to protect land and water.

The unselfconscious everyday lives of these friends show clearly what Paul called the fruit of the spirit.

> *The fruit of the Spirit is love, joy, peace, longsuffering, gentleness, goodness, faith, meekness, temperance. Against such things there is no law (Gal. 5:22-23 KJV).*

Fruit is food—nourishing and sweet. These friends have strengthened my spirit as they demonstrate each of these virtues.

FORGIVENESS

I've had relationships in which one of us failed in this strengthening. When someone behaves consistently in a disrespectful manner without apparent regret, it may be best to sever the tie, but such a loss is painful. It hurts because love doesn't end, and because both parties may have a role in the failure. When I see I was at fault, the pain is coupled with guilt. But in these cases the possibility of forgiveness exists and can repair the spiritual damage for whichever party is willing to access it, injured or injurer. Sometimes, to reduce harm, physical and emotional separation is necessary, but the spiritual tie is unbreakable. Even years later or after the loved one has died, we can go into the place where forgiveness awaits. In my life sometimes many changes must occur within me before I can align with this virtue, especially with regard to forgiving myself.

WE CAN BE INSPIRED BY WRITINGS THAT ILLUMINATE GOODNESS

Sometimes the eternal verities come to us most vividly through books or films, and for serious seekers, it's a common event for the right text to come to hand at the right time. "When the student is ready, the teacher will appear" is a saying attributed variously to Buddha and the tradition of Tibetan Buddhism, the Tao Te Ching, and Zen proverbs.

From childhood until today I don't remember a twenty-four-hour period when I didn't have a book in hand or nearby, ready for the next reading opportunity. Books were my escape, but as I reached adulthood they were also the best means I had for learning. During the years when my children were small, I read only non-fiction, which suited my interests and could fit the short blocks of time I had free. I was looking for truth about the biggest, most basic questions humans can ask. I wanted to find out what thoughtful people believed about the nature of reality — ontology — sometimes referred to as the science of being.

SEEKING TRUTH IN NON-FICTION

I read the books my then-husband brought home from his classes at seminary and university. I read theologians, but without much satisfaction. I read psychology, beginning with Freud. I was feeling my way toward a view of the world for which I lacked words. What I could say, however, was "I don't see a difference between sacred and secular."

I began to find what I was looking for years later when in my local public library I came across a shelf containing Library of Congress codes B (Philosophy, Psychology, Religion), BC (Logic), and BD (Speculative philosophy). One of the first books the section gave me was cultural historian Morris Berman's 1989 classic *Coming to Our Senses*. In it he points to a fault in Western culture: denial of the body. He argues for reuniting body and spirit, which somehow even then I recognized as my own protest. At the time I was puzzled by his critique of the fourth-century decision by the Church to elevate Jesus's divinity above his humanity, but I knew Berman was advocating a worldview that was whole rather than split into categories.[24]

The book set me on a reading path that has never come to an end. I went from one book to another in that section, and I read titles these authors referred to, such as *Wholeness and the Implicate Order* by theoretical physicist David Bohm (which I kept at hand by making extensive photocopies, as this was a period in which I couldn't afford to buy books). Bohm sees in quantum physics a clear demonstration that spiritual and physical are not separate categories. What he calls an "implicate" order exists within the more visible world that he calls "explicate." Although much of his thinking was beyond my grasp, I could nonetheless recognize that he was dealing with my concerns.

> *Man's general way of thinking of the totality, i.e. his general world view, is crucial for overall order of the human mind itself. If he thinks of the totality as constituted of independent fragments, then that is how his mind will tend to operate, but if he can include everything coherently and harmoniously in an overall whole that is undivided, unbroken and without border (for every border is a division or break) then his mind will tend to move in a similar way, and from this will flow an orderly action within the whole.*[25]

What I wanted was a worldview that incorporated "everything coherently and harmoniously in an overall whole that is undivided, unbroken and without border." Until I read writers such as Berman and Bohm, I didn't know I was questioning the dualism of Western culture—the reductionist philosophy that has made possible the path of destruction we're now on. They gave me language and opened a door, and I am very grateful.

FINDING VIRTUE IN FICTION

Of course truth is found not only in non-fiction, and not only in literature written for adults. For an understanding of kindness I couldn't have found a better guide than *Wind in the Willows* by Kenneth Grahame. In this tale I enter with Mole into the riverside world of Rat (actually a European water vole). I am present during their first tentative conversations, when shy Mole with awed exclamations examines Rat's delightful boat and the well-stocked picnic basket. Wise Ratty becomes Mole's guide and companion in above-ground adventures. He rescues Mole from terror in the wild wood and introduces him to the daunting personage of Badger as well as the audacious and reckless Toad. When inadvertently they come near Mole's old hole in the ground—the home that had once seemed fine and precious but which now he fears to expose to the eyes of his more worldly and prosperous new friend—Ratty is a model of astute tact and tenderness toward his protégé.

Throughout this handbook I quote from *Lord of the Rings* by J.R.R. Tolkien, one of the most-loved books of our era. In the text I find parallels for many of the situations we are now facing, and I'm stirred by the valor and virtue of its characters. I'm inspired by Aragorn, who prepares sixty years for his kingship; by Gandalf, who returns from sacrificial death to complete his Third Age mission; and by Frodo and Sam, who persist in the near-hopeless quest despite the fiercest hardship. Merry and Pippin remain true through many ordeals, as do the elf Legolas and the dwarf Gimli. The excellent Faramir holds to his values in the face of his father's scorn, and Beregond risks punishment of death to save his captain from the fire of madness.

And all of these, as well as Eowyn, whose strength rises as steel to protect her beloved king and kinsman Theoden, exemplify loyalty and love. Here men shed tears, embrace freely, and speak openly of their feelings for each other and for their people. These defenders of the West of that island are bound together by affection as well as policy. The fact that war and fighting are part of the drama reflects the reality of our way of life. I'd rather read of heroes who are not called upon to draw a sword, but these are the legends of our heritage.

(For more books on my reading path, *see* Appendix I.)

WE CAN DEMONSTRATE GOODNESS IN OUR OWN BEHAVIOR

> *A virtue is not just a positive quality that makes you a better human being. The virtue is the agency in something. It's a power to act. When the old alchemists used to talk about the virtue of lead or the virtue of sulfur or the virtue of gold, they weren't just talking about how good it was. They were talking about the thing in it that is the principle that makes it work. And so when we talk about faith, hope, love, peace, gentleness, patience, forbearance, these are action agents. They are the power to act, and human beings are required to be virtuous in order to act in the world in the way nature has appointed for us. When we are being compassionate, we are exercising the agency of compassion, and through that exercise we are putting that virtue, that beautiful nutrient into the world.*
>
> CYNTHIA BOURGEAULT[26]

The eternal verities have stirred my imagination toward actions I otherwise would not have chosen. I can feel their agency working to change me toward their purposes. When I say "I pursue the truth," I realize it's more that truth is pursuing me. Truth is tugging at me, moving me toward being more truthful. Fairness is telling me to be more fair. They are powers as well as principles.

Exercising the agency of fairness

The major injustice I witnessed every day as I grew up in the southern United States in the late 1930s and early 1940s was racial inequality. Seventy percent of the county population was Black; Black people were in sight wherever I went. They lived on our property and worked in my home and the homes of my friends, and yet their wants and needs didn't matter to their employers. Politically and socially they had no standing in the dominant White culture. As a child I yearned to have the power to act on their behalf. Bourgeault's words tell me that in some way my compassion helped the world repair this overwhelming breach of justice.

RECOGNIZING UNFAIR ADVANTAGE

I knew I was advantaged by my Whiteness and by almost every other indicator of status. By the good fortune of having been born to parents who could provide well for my physical needs, education, and social training, doors opened without my having to knock. I was uncomfortable with the inequalities then, and in the second half of my life I've spent most of my time and money supporting efforts toward systemic change.

But our spiritual teachers set a very high standard regarding societal privilege. St. Francis of Assisi took a vow of poverty. The Buddha renounced his family's wealth to be a wandering ascetic. Jesus, when approached by the rich young ruler, said, "Sell whatsoever thou hast, and give to the poor" (Mark 10:21 KJV). Jesus and his disciples were not from the prosperous classes, and neither were most of the humans who've ever lived, nor most who live today. Affluence is uncommon. The most remarkable thing about being a middle-class American at this time is this: while by US Census Bureau measurement we are not wealthy, by global standards we are, and our position is clearly unjust. By that I mean not only do we have disproportionate wealth, but the wealth we have is ill-gotten.

The coal, oil, gas, uranium, lumber, soil, and waters Europeans took by violence from the American Indian have served as the basis of our nation's success since the Pilgrims landed here in 1620. Between Independence and the Civil War it was primarily the forced labor of enslaved Africans in cotton fields by which the United States became the second biggest industrial power in the world.[27] And from the time our country grew into an economic empire until today, probably not an area of the planet exists that has not given up its treasures to one or more US multinational corporations, whose products Americans have then bought. Those who are doing well now have inherited benefits that gave us leverage to add value by our own efforts.

After seeing that injustice has occurred and that I have benefited from it, I might remain paralyzed by guilt. But I'm choosing instead a course that seems more useful: to enter into a state of active compassion for all victims, and to lend my hand to improve the structures that do harm.

Nevertheless I'm still challenged when I read what Jesus said when the rich young ruler asked, "What shall I do that I may inherit eternal life?" In the language of my concerns I would ask, "What must I do to live by the principle of fairness, or justice?" Looking at today's troubles, at the top of the list is nature—all the environmental crises that put Earth life unequally in peril. As a consumer in a consumer society, what can I do to reduce my load on the planet? If I could give a fearless answer to that one question, I could put my influence toward the greatest injustice of the human era: the destruction of the basis for life, which falls with undue weight on those who are least responsible and the least able to bear it.

QUESTIONING CONSUMER BEHAVIOR

To make the answers more obvious, I will reverse the perspective: which of my unjust actions—representing behavior that harms the ecosystem—are absolutely beyond my ability to correct? Seen from that view, the list grows shorter. I think of our car. It gets over fifty miles to the gallon, we bought it used and it is now ten years old, I rarely drive except to medical appointments and church, and yet . . . could I do without a car? I live in a rural area with no public transportation, but I have friends with cars. Could I do without a car? Of course I could.

The internet is a major energy hog. I don't mean the electricity that runs my personal laptop or wireless access, but the draw of the enormous data server installations powering internet searches. Could I do the research for this book without the web? Perhaps, and I do use books when possible. I could access the internet on the computer at the library, though I would need a car to get there. But could I manage my life without the internet? Of course.

In fact I'm writing this book for people who within their lifetimes may not have cars or web access, and I'm telling them, as I truly believe, that life can still be good. It will be different, but it will become less harmful to living things and that will be satisfying to me, and I think to many readers. And ahead of the necessity, I want to move step by step toward a life that doesn't consume Earth's treasures or produce waste. Just as I've contributed to the harm by my consumption, so I now want to contribute to the repair to the extent of my power.

WITHDRAWING SUPPORT FROM AN UNFAIR SYSTEM

Regarding the unjust climate policies of my nation and state, it seems that producing significant change is not in my power at this time. Therefore to the extent of my body's abilities and my time not spent on immediate needs, I can pursue the only goal that makes sense now, given the political situation: withdraw as much as I can from this ruinous system. Taking the bitter with the sweet, I can accept the pain of rejecting more of industrialism's benefits in order to make possible a better life for those who follow.

I can plant trees that are suitable to grow here now and after this area is far warmer. I can improve the soil so that this land has a better chance to support life in the coming decades—plant or animal, domesticated or wild. I can look for a high-level official or influencer who is willing to talk about degrowth if not deindustrialization. In conversation but also in public forums I can speak about the reality few people have the chance to understand: future life depends on reducing our load to nature's carrying capacity.

What is beyond my power to do in order to further fairness on the personal level? As individuals, few of us have the resources to support even one family fleeing climate disaster. Yet the great teachers have told us the danger of holding onto possessions. Or rather, their examples teach that possessions interfere with the spirit of life—the sense of being alive in this precious world. A light hold on belongings has always been helpful to happiness as well as a benefit to others, but the sense of "the party's over" now makes generosity more pressing. The time to invest in someone else's well-being is now, while I have the resources to do it.

RELEASING ATTACHMENT TO BENEFITS

In *Lord of the Rings,* as Frodo and Samwise approach Mount Doom and the end of their quest, Sam takes stock of the distance and their state of exhaustion.

> *As he worked things out, slowly a new dark thought grew in his mind. . . . The bitter truth came home to him at last; at best their provision would take them to their goal; and when the task was done, there they would come to an end, alone, houseless, foodless in the midst of a terrible desert. . . . He pointed to the Mountain. "It's no good taking anything we're not sure to need." He took out all the things in his pack. Somehow each of them had become dear to him if only because he had borne them so far with so much toil. Hardest of all it was to part with his cooking-gear. Tears welled in his eyes at the thought of casting it away.*[28]

My heart tells me it is time to release attachment to anything I don't really need. If the house is on fire, you get out and bring with you the other living creatures and, if you planned for emergencies, your go-bag and some cash. There is growing disorder in the world around me. I feel the logic of shedding attachments in order to focus on things money can't buy.

> *Let yourself be silently drawn by the strange pull of what you really love. It will not lead you astray.*
>
> RUMI[29]

For reasons that I hope this account has made clear, my life has been oriented toward fairness more than almost any other virtue. In some ways the effort to be fair in my dealings is the most challenging goal I could have chosen, especially in these times of highly visible global-scale inequality. The burden would be less heavy if I didn't know about our predicament and my involvement, but if I didn't know, I would be less helpful, and someone else's heaviness might be even greater. I look upon the knowing as a way to share a small part of the suffering, and perhaps to offer a bit of relief.

> *The Fourth Precept of the Order of Interbeing tells us to be aware of suffering in the world, not to close our eyes before suffering. Touching those who suffer is one way to generate the energy of compassion in us, and compassion will bring joy and peace to ourselves and others.*
>
> THICH NHAT HANH[30]

Exercising the agency of truth

> *Ye shall know the truth and the truth shall set you free.*
>
> JOHN 8:32 KJV

If there is an eternal verity that has seized me with a force equal to that of fairness, it would be truth. My quest to understand the nature of reality—ontology—was the first conscious and persistent pursuit of truth in my life. The Western world has divided reality into physical and spiritual, and since only the physical can be reliably demonstrated, politics and science operate as if only the physical exists. I've described the reading path by which my doubts about the reductionist theory came to be validated and my belief in the unity of nature and spirit affirmed.

TRUTH-SEEKING IN PERSONAL HISTORY

When I was in my fifties I entered the second stage of my pursuit of truth. While sitting on my sofa one afternoon with a notebook on my lap, this thought hit me: I will find out, looking back into my childhood, that what I have believed to be white was actually black, and what I have believed to be black was white. The words of the premonition turned out to be as accurate as language is capable of being, and on that afternoon, despite the fear I felt, I chose to open to the truth rather than go on believing a fantasy.

I had not reached mid-life unaware that mysterious chains limited my choices. I was torn between doing what others thought I should do and following the small, feeble voice that was my true inclination. As a teenager I had not rebelled. Within the space of my mind I held to my own views and acknowledged my feelings, but outwardly I conformed to my parents' expectations. After I left home their hold on me was almost as strong as ever; I merely found surrogates whose opinions guided my actions. I believed doctors, older relatives, and my husband were more powerful than I could be, and though I struggled consciously to voice my own desires rather than fit smoothly into the social pattern, my will to act was weaker than my fears. Even after I became a mother and felt I had to speak up on behalf of my children, I compromised.

It was not until I found what Alice Miller calls "an enlightened witness" to my dilemma that I could begin to dissolve the unconscious bonds. In 1997 in an essay explaining the behavior of well-known criminals, Miller wrote, "Information about abuse inflicted during childhood is recorded in our body cells as a sort of memory, linked to repressed anxiety. If, lacking the aid of an enlightened witness, these memories fail to break through to consciousness, they often compel the person to violent acts that reproduce the abuse suffered in childhood, which was repressed in order to survive."[31] The explanation also applies to submissive behavior.

My enlightened witness was Miller's assurance that I could trust the small glimpses of truth that sometimes broke into consciousness, and I followed those glimpses until I learned the truth of my personal history.

TRUTH-TELLING IN PUBLIC ADVOCACY

A third aspect of my effort to follow the principle of Truth is my political path—my work for justice in societal and governmental structures. Recently the relationship of fairness and truth has become far more evident. In the months since the very public endorsement of fascist methods to gain power in January 2021 by US leaders at the highest levels of electoral office, truth has been at the center of the struggle. As I write, those of us who are resisting the culture of lies and distortion are on the defensive; our voices are indistinct compared with the volume and violence of far-right messaging. Although people with my views compose a majority of our nation's population, we now seem to be the resistance rather than the rule. We had hoped democratic traditions and aspirational ideals would carry enough weight to overcome the structural deficiencies of founding documents and legal patterns, but a forty-year neoliberal campaign to protect the wealthy while confusing the public has claimed the stage.

Truth nevertheless is still the strength of those who advocate for life. Vaclav Havel, later the first president of the Czech Republic but who in 1968 was merely a well-known playwright and dissident, wrote at that time about the importance of the young underground musicians who called themselves The Plastic People of the Universe.

> *The world is beautiful*
> *But plastic people don't see it.*
> *Flowers are beautiful*
> *But plastic people don't see it.*
> *The sunset is beautiful*
> *But plastic people don't see it.*[32]

Arrested as layabouts and hooligans because of their desire "to express themselves in a truthful way," this rock-and-roll group became the point of an arrow piercing the blind acceptance of dictatorship by the Czech people. As a result of the government's persecution of this group, Czechoslovakians recognized what was being lost as they conformed to expectations. Havel's famous essay, "The Power of the Powerless," which can be viewed as a treatise on truth, tells how a nation woke up to what only a few had been saying. Reading these words encourages me to speak my dissent more loudly: "The singular, explosive, incalculable political power of living within the truth resides in the fact that living openly within the truth has an ally, invisible to be sure, but omnipresent . . . the human predisposition to truth."[33]

Havel's words encourage me. May the human predisposition to truth overcome the insistent, deceitful messaging in which a good part of our citizenry is immersed. May it manifest strongly in my own life. For if, as I believe, important information—about climate change, for example—is not being conveyed in a helpful way by mass media, don't those who keep up with the science have a growing responsibility to fill that gap?

At the moment I think the most useful way to explain our imperilment and the need for change is to describe what sustainability means from the perspective of nature. Nature has seemed so tolerant up to now that few actually know the boundaries we face. The truth is that fitting in with nature's plan is the only way humans will be able to survive. And if people don't know what nature's plan allows, how can they be motivated to endorse the needed changes?

The truth is we face a much broader peril than global warming. What news stories are calling species extinction, widespread toxicity, and heat domes is really evidence of ecosystem collapse. Shouldn't I be offering that information widely, informally as well as through public advocacy? To sustain life on this planet we must live as the planet decrees. In nature there is no depletion of what we call resources, and no waste. Period. That simple standard cuts through the morass of so-called solutions that might keep the machines running but fail to keep humans on the Earth. That's the imperative by which we can measure our conduct, and it is the standard we can set for public policy.

And the standard for advocacy has also been described by Vaclav Havel: "Living within the truth . . . (is) an attempt to regain control over one's own sense of responsibility. In other words, it is clearly a moral act, not only because one must pay so dearly for it, but principally because it is not self-serving: the risk may bring rewards in the form of a general amelioration in the situation, or it may not."[34]

Living within the truth is a moral act, and it is a spiritual power whether or not it is rewarded in the visible realm. I have a responsibility—I have the moral obligation—to go public with my understanding about the dangers we face as an aspiringly democratic nation and also as a species that would like to survive. My views on both subjects might be considered subversive by powerful forces, though at this time neither is likely to make me a target of the authorities. Truth, however, is not friendly to oppressors of any variety, and as things get more dire, who can say what price truth-tellers may come to pay?

FINE POINTS OF TRUTH-SEEKING AND TRUTH-TELLING

Being truthful as I took a position against the view known as reductionism was perfectly safe. Being truthful about my family of origin didn't feel safe, but I could protect myself by establishing distance when I needed it. Being truthful out loud in public to protest the directions my country is taking could pose physical danger I might not be able to prevent. I hope I will always be as bold as the occasion demands.

I hope I will also be as cautious as courtesy calls for. My purpose is not to make others ashamed of a less strenuous commitment. Neither should I be the teller of a truth that could fracture someone's hold on self-possession. Further, I must acknowledge my own fallibility. The fact that each of the men associated with reductionist views I see as false was engaged in a sincere search for truth gives me caution: Plato, Hobbs, Descartes, de Laplace, Weinberg, and Dawkins, to name only a few. If these great thinkers could be mistaken, so could I.

Jeremy Lent warns that "excessive self-control, impulsiveness or zealous attachment to a belief system can all work against the 'democracy of consciousness' that would aid decision-making by taking advantage of the different aspects of the self."[35] When I am trying to decide if something is true, an internal dialogue is going on, some of it outside of awareness. If I honor all aspects of myself, in time the internal "democracy" will have a chance to arrive at the best possible conclusion, based on the information in hand at the moment.

In 1959 the BBC asked Bertrand Russell what advice he would give future generations. He answered, "When you are studying any matter or considering any philosophy, ask yourself only what are the facts and what is the truth that the facts bear out. Never let yourself be diverted either by what you wish to believe or by what you think would have been beneficent social effects if it were believed, but look only and solely at what are the facts."[36]

I have made an effort to do that, with the questioning about larger reality, with my personal history, and with my public voice about the perils of our times. In the coming days, as chaos gains on order, and confusion mounts due to compounding adversity, truth-seeking can only become more difficult, and truth-telling more precarious.

Whenever I am considering whether a thing is true, I can check off these practices:

- Be honest with myself
- Expect that others will be honest most of the time
- Ask relevant questions or otherwise seek more information
- Give my "democracy of consciousness" a chance to assemble these factors and reach a judgment
- Remain humble, recognizing that I do make mistakes
- Respect the right of another to come to a conclusion that contradicts what appears to me to be reasonable.

But appropriate humility doesn't prevent bold declaration. Like the Wise Men who followed the star until it stood over the stable in Bethlehem (Matt. 2:9 KJV), I aspire to follow truth wherever it takes me. The more confusing or threatening things become, the more diligently I hope to pursue it.

IN CONCLUSION

Spiritual practices that give us strength are useful in either prosperity or adversity. They are important now, however, not only to see us through a hard period, but also to lead us toward new ways of living. For more than three centuries the Western world has been immersed in the view that spirit—if such a thing existed—would have nothing to do with the hard realities that could be demonstrated in a laboratory. The heart of the human has been pushed into the background by commercial interests, practical science, and even by much religious doctrine.

If societal disruption is to become a transition into a more sustainable era rather than a termination of *Homo sapiens*, I think we will need to focus on the positive ideals that point to the nature of the universe. We must live by them, talk about them with others, and circulate the wisdom of present-day teachers whose guidance will add momentum to the shift.

At this time powerful people are forcing destruction upon us, unconcerned about our welfare. They may be blinded by the pursuit of money, or they may be numbed from the lack of spiritual guidance. Whether they are unmindful or filled with malevolent intentionality, their effect is deadly. I avoid dwelling on their motives. What I seek out is proper food for bringing my spirit in line with the beauty of the benevolent Earth. I find it in words, images, and people that demonstrate what is good. That search is validated in the Beatitudes attributed to Jesus in the book of Matthew, in the statement "Blessed are they which do hunger and thirst after righteousness (living in right relationship), for they shall be filled" (Matt. 5:5 KJV). In this writing I hope to increase awareness of a hunger and a thirst for the ideals that are food for our spirits.

Among the last words Jesus is said to have spoken is the following text:

> Let not your heart be troubled: ye believe in God, believe also in me. In my Father's house are many mansions: if it were not so, I would have told you. I go to prepare a place for you.
>
> And if I go and prepare a place for you, I will come again, and receive you unto myself; that where I am, there ye may be also.
>
> JOHN 14: 2–3 KJV

This is figurative language, and in my view it relates as much to what we can see now as it does to an afterlife. In the quiet of my soul through the windows of the eternal verities, I may look into the many mansions of the life in which we are held. What our spirits can show us in this life is enough to make us strong. Whatever death holds will be seamless with the wonders already available to us.

Two of the last sightings of Bachman's warbler, recently declared extinct, were of lone males singing from the high perches once favored by this species. No bird was heard to answer, and no mate may have ever responded in the experience of either singer. Nevertheless the songs continued, for singing is what birds do. In this writing I have described a very personal way I've found that nurtures my spirit in the direction nature seems to have intended. Anchored by the eternal verities and by the symbols that speak of them to my imagination, I hope to do what humans are meant to do: live joyfully to the end.

> If you put your heart against the earth with me,
> in serving every creature,
> our Beloved will enter you from our sacred realm
> and we will be, we will be
> so happy.
>
> RUMI[37]

In this handbook I've described a perhaps uniquely applicable practice that shapes me and feeds my spirit. I found it intuitively—who can say how?—and it has served me well for eight decades of a journey that was sometimes difficult but nevertheless fortuitously guided. I needed more than the original discovery to reach the peace I now enjoy, but overall I have followed the thread.

> *There's a thread you follow. It goes among*
> *things that change. But it doesn't change.*
> *People wonder about what you are pursuing.*
> *You have to explain about the thread.*
> *But it is hard for others to see.*
> *While you hold it you can't get lost.*
> *Tragedies happen; people get hurt*
> *or die; and you suffer and get old.*
> *Nothing you do can stop time's unfolding.*
> *You don't ever let go of the thread.*
>
> WILLIAM STAFFORD[38]

The thread I have followed has many manifestations. I introduced the eternal verities by mentioning fairness, goodness, beauty, and truth. I quoted Wendell Berry's list: truth, mercy, justice, forgiveness, peace, equality, trust, hospitality, generosity, freedom, love, neighborliness, home, reverence, beauty, care, courtesy, goodness, faith, kindness, health, wholeness, holiness.

I described how a teacher had exemplified kindness, and four friends have shown me integrity, loyalty, sacrifice, and justice. I said the virtue of forgiveness heals when friendship fails.

I quoted Paul, whose fruits of the spirit include things that are true, things that are honest, things that are just, things that are pure, things that are lovely, things that are of good report.

I quoted Tolkien, whose elves sang of the Blessed Realm with clear melody and voice, and whose hobbits valued the elves, the stars, the trees, and the gentle fall of the bright year in the woods.

I related the story of the wolf inside us who could be fed peace, love, hope, humility, kindness, generosity, and compassion. I found truth in my non-fiction reading trail; as I read fiction I found courtesy, tenderness, fidelity, and love. I described how in my own life I've pursued fairness and truth.

I could add other wonders that bring goodness to mind: flowers, trumpets, babies, bells. Sun on the moving surface of a lake. Music. We must each find the things that stir our own spirits to greater life, and then we must take time to give them our full attention. I offer my practice as a possible path for others to explore.

HANDBOOK TWO

Deepening Our Connections With Other Humans and the Rest of Nature

NOW IS THE TIME FOR HUMANS TO REALIZE OUR UNITY WITH ALL OTHER HUMANS AND WITH NATURE — AND DEEPEN OUR CONNECTIONS WITH BOTH.

Handbook Two

Deepening Our Connections With Other Humans and the Rest of Nature

Contents

WE CAN BEGIN BY UNDERSTANDING OUR EVOLUTIONARY NATURE / 52

   Some human traits interfere with connection / 53
- THERE MAY BE SUSPICION TOWARD CULTURAL STRANGERS / 53
- WE MAY SEE THE FOLLOWING ORDERS SYNDROME / 54
- THERE MAY BE AGGRESSIVE CONDUCT TO RELEASE TENSION OR DOMINATE / 54

   Humans have a long history of communal living / 55
- HUNTER-GATHERER CULTURE WAS EGALITARIAN / 55
- THERE IS AUTONOMY IN EGALITARIAN SOCIETIES / 56
- EGOISM, NEPOTISM, AND ALTRUISM FUNCTION TOGETHER / 56
- INDIVIDUAL POWER DEPENDS ON A UNIFIED COLLECTIVE / 57

WE CAN EXAMINE THE IMPACT OF CULTURE ON OUR HUMAN NATURE / 58

   We can learn to depend on the strength of the collective / 60

   Communal cultures can teach us village-mindedness / 61

   We have come to the heart of the matter / 63

WE CAN UNDO THE CONDITIONING THAT KEEPS US IN SHALLOW RELATIONSHIPS / 64

   Adulthood is not too late to become more open / 65

   We can learn life-supporting communication / 67
- WE CAN OBSERVE WITHOUT EVALUATING / 67
- WE CAN LEARN: I OBSERVE, I FEEL, I NEED, AND I WANT / 68
- WE CAN VIEW EVERY ACT AS AN ATTEMPT TO MEET NEEDS / 68

   We can practice non-attachment / 69

WE CAN LEARN WHAT IT MEANS TO LIVE WITHIN COMMUNITY / 70

   To co-operate is to operate with equal authority / 73

   The boys show us how it's done / 73

   Community is hindered by our language / 74

   We can take small steps toward community / 76

IN CONCLUSION / 79

The problems our society faces are immense and complex. My path through complexity is to look for fundamental causes, and in my view the absence of deep connections underlies most of the problems.

> The perception that humans are more worthy than the rest of nature—loss of connection—has resulted in a way of life that harms nature.

> The perception that some humans are more worthy than other humans—loss of connection—has resulted in a way of life that harms other humans.

To repair the harms, humans must realize our unity with all other humans and with nature—and deepen our connections with both. Yet here we are, considering the need for connectedness and unity at a time when disunity and disconnection seem to grow almost daily. In the United States, we've seen division sown loudly and intentionally with amazing success in recent years, headline after headline, day after day. For the campaign of division to be this successful indicates an existing condition that merely had to be exploited. We were ripe to be divided because too many of us already thought of ourselves as separate—from each other and from the rest of nature.

I can remember where I was when I first read that I was not a separate being. At the time it was an idea that seemed far-fetched and irrelevant. Yet it stayed in my mind so firmly that when I reached the same understanding in my own way, I realized I had finally grasped the meaning of those words by Alan Watts that I had read thirty years earlier. For thirty years a part of my mind had held onto the idea until the rational part of me became able to understand it.

It is no wonder it took me so long. Connectedness is not a rational comprehension. Belonging together is a condition to be learned by experience, as when a child belongs to its mother, its family, its home. If I had grown up in a culture that saw humans as part of each other and of nature, I wouldn't have needed to have the connection explained. It would have been an experience deeper than logic, a tie that, like family, would have been difficult to sever.

How do we begin to learn unity when we haven't experienced much of it? How do we undo the misconceptions that I'm saying are at the root of our environmental, social, spiritual, and economic problems?

In this handbook we will consider four strategies to restore our sense of connection with other humans and with more-than-human nature:

(1) We can begin by understanding our evolutionary characteristics. Are humans fitted for harmony with others and with the whole life family?

(2) We can examine our cultural heritage. Who have we been shaped to become?

(3) We can work to undo the conditioning that keeps us in shallow relationships. How do we deepen them?

(4) We can learn what it means to live within community.

In Handbook One, Strengthening Our Spirits, I voiced my fear that entering this period of uncertainty, many of my contemporaries are ill-equipped regarding spiritual strength. I have no less concern about the depth of our communality. I'm not as inhibited when speaking of ways to strengthen our spirits, however, since the path I described is one I have lived for eight decades. When I write about connectedness, I'm speaking of something I've only begun to learn.

But there is another reason I'm more cautious about recommending that a person move toward others as a way to manage this era of chaos. I can promise that when a person reaches inward for support, unseen forces are ever present to help us within the scope of their powers on the spiritual plane. I cannot promise that the people we reach toward in the more visible world will be ready to befriend us in return. As a shrinking economy takes away people's employment, as environmental disasters move people from their homes and threaten food supplies, and as institutions that have served to keep order either fail, or themselves become agencies of violence, we may be trying to build community with people too distressed to respond.

The more tense the atmosphere becomes, however, the more important it will be to make these connections. Safety doesn't lie in the direction of greater isolation. In this handbook I emphasize the genetic and cultural factors in human nature so that we may see our neighbors more accurately. And I offer training in social interaction so that we may reach out to them with more grace and skill. Every bridge we build offers a chance for greater security for ourselves today, and these bridges—even if we don't get to cross over on them—may serve those who come after us.

WE CAN BEGIN BY UNDERSTANDING OUR EVOLUTIONARY NATURE

Hear the words of Etty Hillesum from her diary in the German concentration camp where she died:

> *I am not easily frightened. Not because I am brave but because I know that I am dealing with human beings, and that I must try as hard as I can to understand everything that anyone ever does. And that was the real import of this morning: not that a disgruntled young Gestapo officer yelled at me, but that I felt no indignation, rather a real compassion, and would have liked to ask, "Did you have a very unhappy childhood, has your girlfriend let you down?" Yes, he looked harassed and driven, sullen and weak. I should have liked to start treating him there and then, for I know that pitiful young men like that are dangerous as soon as they are let loose on mankind.*[39]

She was right in seeing that people can be dangerous. Yet she was also right to recognize that the people she was surrounded by were nevertheless only human beings—shaped by their experiences, but with a common genetic character.

We are all human. The humans I meet, while each is unique, are the result of an ancestry we share. All the people of our world were formed in the deeps of time by the same evolutionary process. Anatomically modern *Homo sapiens* has been present on planet Earth for 300,000 years.[40] For almost all that time we survived as what anthropologists call immediate-return hunter gatherers, meaning we lived on current, not stored, food supplies. During this period we evolved the basic traits that make us human. We traveled in small bands where virtues like altruism, sharing, and the preservation of nature were essential to group survival. Our societies were sustainable and egalitarian. We still have it in us to live that way. We are human.

For several decades scientists have been documenting, through experiments and close examination of real-life events, that *Homo sapiens* from the first months of life is oriented toward helpfulness and cooperation. In 2020 Brian Hare and Vanessa Woods, both researchers at Duke University's Center for Cognitive Neuroscience, published *The Survival of the Friendliest: Understanding Our Origins and Rediscovering*

Our Common Humanity. In it they conclude, "Cooperation is the key to our survival as a species because it increases our evolutionary fitness." They say, "What allowed us to thrive while other humans went extinct was a kind of cognitive superpower: a particular type of friendliness called cooperative communication. We are experts at working together with other people, even strangers. We can communicate with someone we've never met about a shared goal and work together to accomplish it. . . . We develop all these skills before we can walk or talk, and they are the gateway to a sophisticated social and cultural world."[41]

A quick look at the large number of positive results when searching on a phrase such as "cooperation and human evolution" shows that academics are confirming this view and looking for the likely explanations. These scientists are asking, "How did the traits of friendliness and cooperative behavior come to be so characteristic of humans?" rather than "Are humans cooperative?". It's the same question Darwin puzzled over: why "human degrees of generosity seem to defy the patently 'selfish' principles of natural selection theory."[42]

Some human traits interfere with connection

In global society at the present time, however, the puzzlement is more often about the conflict that seems characteristic of individuals and groups. Etty Hillesum's description of the young Gestapo officer, and the reminder that she died in a Nazi concentration camp, seem all too like the news coming to our attention today. Are there factors in our heredity that account for war, for economic conflict, and for ordinary, everyday cruelties? Certainly. Humans have inherited a wide array of tendencies, and some of them may lean away from friendliness.

THERE MAY BE SUSPICION TOWARD CULTURAL STRANGERS

Etty Hillesum was interned because she was Jewish. When leaders or group of elites aim to divide the community by naming certain traits as "bad" or as the cause of troubles, humans may respond by lowering the status of members with those characteristics.

In the United States we continue to deal with this challenge to egalitarianism. Legal structures as well as individual bias continue to target American Indians, African Americans whose ancestors were brought here enslaved, and other non-White people, especially those of Asian descent, Muslims and others from the Near East, and those migrating from south of the border. Such policies lend authority to negative judgments. They make it easier for people in these groups to be mistreated.

Respected evolutionary anthropologist Christopher Boehm observes, "... our moral codes apply fully only within the group, be it a language group, a non-literate population that shares the same piece of real estate or the same ethnic identity, or a nation. There seems to be a special, pejorative 'discount' applied to cultural strangers."[43]

Yet with exposure, people often cease to be strangers. With familiarity, categories of race or religion—or blue eyes[44]—or any other means of classification stop being a signal of lower value. In the United States, it is the zip codes with the least diversity that tend to vote against measures that promote it, and the farther people live from the southern border of the nation, the more they favor building a wall to keep immigrants out.[45]

WE MAY SEE THE FOLLOWING ORDERS SYNDROME

Another human tendency that may be seen in the Etty Hillesum example is the "following orders" syndrome. Experiments have shown that when people act under orders, they seem to experience less responsibility for their actions and outcomes than when they choose for themselves.[46] This is one of many negative features of hierarchic arrangements.

THERE MAY BE AGGRESSIVE CONDUCT TO RELEASE TENSION OR DOMINATE

The Hillesum account also mentions the tendency for a person to resolve internal anxiety through aggressive conduct. There have always been a few in every population, too, whose leaning toward aggression is so consistent as to seem almost inborn.[47] And then there are those who simply take advantage of opportunity, using charm or force to gain an undue amount of power. Groups, small or large, must find ways to discourage aggressive individuals, and to separate the violent from potential victims.

As I'm reading reports from anthropologists who lived among hunter-gatherer groups long enough to gain their trust, I keep noticing the effort it takes to preserve the power-sharing arrangement most of the group members prefer. It seems common that male members will reach for power over others and will have to be restrained by the rest of the group. American anthropologist Bruce Knaupf writes, "To control someone who tries to dominate other group members or to misuse a position of status, group members may ridicule, walk away, disobey, or simply ignore that individual. Other tactics are to rebuke, rebel against, remove, ostracize or expel an over-assertive individual from the group, and in extreme cases execution is also an option."[48]

Tomazho, a wise Ju/'hoan healer, explained to Richard Lee, who spent years with the Ju/'hoansi in Africa: "When a young man kills much meat, he comes to think of himself as a big man, and he thinks of the rest of us as his inferiors. We can't accept this. We refuse one who boasts, for someday his pride will make him kill somebody. So we always speak of his meat as worthless. In this way we cool his heart and make him gentle."[49] Indigenous scholar Tyson Yunkaporta of the Apalech clan in Queensland, Australia, says, "Most young men need something a little meatier than mindfulness workshops to curtail the terrifying narcissism that overtakes them from the moment their balls drop."[50]

Humans have a long history of communal living

HUNTER-GATHERER CULTURE WAS EGALITARIAN

Our genetic forebears went to a lot of trouble to maintain self-governance. These hunter-gatherer ancestors insisted on equality of access to basic needs. They knew that the survival of individuals depended on belonging to a group that could survive in the conditions they faced together. There is so much agreement among anthropologists about the egalitarian social structures of early hunter-gatherer history that I would hardly encounter resistance if I should say "it's in our bloodline." Christopher Boehm states simply, "Before twelve thousand years ago, humans basically were egalitarian."[51]

Anthropologists employ the term egalitarian to describe a social arrangement that is somewhat like our term democratic. But while modern democracies elect leaders who then make decisions on our behalf, in a society of pure egalitarians the members themselves make the decisions. James Woodburn, a major hunter-gatherer researcher, writes, "In these societies there are either no leaders at all or leaders who are very elaborately constrained to prevent them exercising authority or using their influence to acquire wealth or prestige."[52]

Knaupf writes that hunter-gatherers of today are still characterized by "extreme political and sexual egalitarianism. Individuals in such groups don't accumulate their own property and possessions. They have a moral obligation to share everything. They also have methods of preserving egalitarianism by ensuring that status differences don't arise."[53]

THERE IS AUTONOMY IN EGALITARIAN SOCIETIES

The term autonomy is also applied to these groups, but it is different from the autonomy of Western individualism. The hunter-gatherers' sense of autonomy is one that connects each person to others, but in a way that does not create dependencies. For example, individuals are free to join a hunting or gathering party or to stay at camp and rest, depending purely on their own preference. This is a freedom that goes far beyond the freedom of most workers in Western culture.[54] In many groups it is extended to women as well as men. Feminist anthropologist and social theorist Eleanor Leacock shares the view that personal autonomy is related to the direct dependence of each individual on the group as a whole. She writes that it is "linked with a way of life that called for great individual initiative and decisiveness along with the ability to be extremely sensitive to the feelings of lodge-mates."[55]

EGOISM, NEPOTISM, AND ALTRUISM FUNCTION TOGETHER

Boehm says humans regularly show three fundamental and competing interests: egoism (care for my own needs), nepotism (care for the needs of relatives), and altruism, or helping behavior beyond the family. He writes that altruistic cooperation "can be greatly culturally amplified in its expression if it is actively and purposefully reinforced by social communities that believe in things like social harmony and the Golden Rule. . . . These intention-bearing inputs are made possible by our large brains."[56]

I view egoism, nepotism, and altruism toward non-kin as a hierarchy of obligation. Our first obligation is to maintain our own gift of life. Then we must also guard the lives of those we bring into our families. But our obligation extends beyond the family to the wider community, too. For self and kin to thrive requires the thriving of the rest of the group. From time to time most of us experience the conflict between these interests, and with our "large brains" we weigh the importance of one or the other obligation in a given setting. But our culture needs to "actively and purposefully" support altruism for it to be prevalent.

INDIVIDUAL POWER DEPENDS ON A UNIFIED COLLECTIVE

Boehm writes that "individuals who would otherwise be subordinated are clever enough to form a large and united political coalition, and they do so for the express purpose of keeping the strong from dominating the weak. Because the united subordinates are constantly putting down the more assertive alpha types in their midst, egalitarianism is in effect a bizarre type of political hierarchy: the weak combine forces to actively dominate the strong. My thesis is that they must continue such domination if they are to remain autonomous and equal, and prehistorically we shall see that they appear to have done so."[57]

Success when resisting domination seems to depend on the unity of the group against the aggressive individual. Yunkaporta writes, "The combination of social fragmentation and lightning-fast communication today, however, means we have to deal with these crazy people alone, as individuals butting heads with narcissists in a lawless void, and they are thriving unchecked in this environment. Engaging with them alone is futile—never wrestle a pig, as the old saying goes; you both end up in shit, and the pig likes it."[58]

The power humans have, in other words, is not as individuals but as a unified collective. If the collective bands together, as they seem to have done in hunter-gatherer groups throughout our long history, no authority figure can overcome them—but vigilance and sometimes strong action are necessary.

And yet there have been groups that were not hunter-gatherers— even cities—that have maintained an egalitarian power structure, sometimes for centuries. David Graeber and David Wengrow have written a 526-page book based on this premise.[59] Their review of the latest archeological studies shows, in their words, "Far from resigning us to inequality, the new picture that is now emerging of humanity's deep past may open our eyes to egalitarian possibilities we otherwise would have never considered." They say, "Where we do have written sources (ancient Mesopotamia, for example), we find large groups of citizens referring to themselves simply as 'the people' of a given city (or often its 'sons'), united by devotion to its founding ancestors, its gods or heroes, its civic infrastructure and ritual calendar."

As one example, they cite Ukrainian cities that endured for eight centuries: "We find little evidence of warfare or the rise of social elites.

The true complexity of these early cities lay in the political strategies they adopted to prevent such things. Careful analysis by archaeologists shows how the social freedoms of the Ukrainian city dwellers were maintained through processes of local decision-making, in households and neighborhood assemblies, without any need for centralized control or top-down administration."[60]

Hierarchies of power happen when people lose faith in each other, and they can be overcome when people regain it. Politics, religion, or financial position may intrude on a person's inclination to trust, but cooperation is our default posture. Since cooperative self-government is a social pattern deep in our history, if we practice cooperative governance in the small groups to which we belong, we may influence individuals who don't yet see the advantage of egalitarian principles.

WE CAN EXAMINE THE IMPACT OF CULTURE ON OUR HUMAN NATURE

The hierarchies that have been the most common societal arrangement for several thousand years have set a pattern that encourages rivalry and distrust. Developments in late seventeenth-century Europe added to the problem, as the philosophers of the Enlightenment upheld individual freedom, and questioned all customs of the past. The industrial economy that began in England and then spread to other nations benefited from this view that individuals were responsible for their own wellbeing. As employers pulled in workers for the mines and looms, they felt free not to be concerned with employees' health or families—whereas formerly landholders and working class had been bound together on the same land for generations, and the profit from this arrangement had depended on a strong and stable workforce.

In industrialized nations many of us lack everyday experience living with great depth of interconnection. But there are still people in North America who have grown up within solid community, and in Zimbabwe I frequently met Africans who, when I said, "Good morning, how are you?" answered, "I'm well if you're well."

Our individualistic culture has isolated us from each other to such an extent that I could answer "I'm fine" speaking as only myself, without acknowledging that this is not possible. It is not possible for me to be fine as an individual if others are not fine. Not only are we not separate from the rest of what we've been taught to call the environment—not only could we not breathe one breath without its presence and support, neither are we, in reality, separate from any other human. For this reason, I believe our preparation for the next period is to acknowledge these ties and to begin to live from this embeddedness.

As I am trying to remember that I am a part of the air, water, and land of Earth, likewise I am trying to be aware that when I rise in the morning, a part of me is in the house of my neighbor, and in some unavailable-to-the-five-senses way, she is in mine. Or something like that. I'm just beginning to try to embody this hitherto-foreign understanding of the depth of my involvement with other humans, as I'm trying to learn to live with nature as part of my being, and myself as part of its circle: "I'm well if you're well."

Hear what Thich Nhat Hanh says in his poem "Please Call Me by My True Names."[61]

> *The rhythm of my heart is the birth and death*
> *of all that are alive.*
> *I am the frog swimming happily*
> *in the clear water of a pond,*
> *and I am the grass-snake*
> *that silently feeds itself on the frog.*
> *I am the twelve-year-old girl,*
> *refugee on a small boat,*
> *who throws herself into the ocean*
> *after being raped by a sea pirate.*
> *And I am the pirate,*
> *my heart not yet capable*
> *of seeing and loving.*

Most Indigenous cultures cultivate a sense of mutual obligation and responsibility in children from a young age. In sub-Saharan Africa the perspective generally known as "ubuntu" (the word for humanity in the Zulu language of South Africa) conveys the sense that "none of the community members would be what he or she is without the community. Thus, naturally the community takes precedence over the individual without underestimating individual personal rights."[62] By contrast Western culture, especially as seen in the United States, asks us to take care of ourselves, regardless of the needs of the community.

We can learn to depend on the strength of the collective

That perspective doesn't stifle the cooperation urge entirely, however, as we see regularly when emergencies arise. We remember how New Yorkers—and many from outside New York—came to the rescue in the events of 9/11, and how hurricanes and fires bring help by strangers from all over the country, no matter where the disasters are located. We share a level of trust in the basic decency of our neighbors and tend to view antisocial behavior as the exception to a general rule.

A fundamental step, then, toward deepening our connections to other people is to recognize that we belong to the whole human community. Connecting in this deep way ought to be the natural course. As humans, we bond with our caregivers almost immediately after birth because in our helpless state we need them to survive. We continue to build ties to those around us even as we grow able to take care of ourselves. Both rationally and emotionally we know we need other people to thrive, and out of that knowledge we form associations that we hope will make us safer and increase our chances for happiness.

I was an American child during World War II, when the strong pull of banding together involved the whole country. In our desks at school we kept war savings bond books in which we pasted war savings stamps, each showing an investment of twenty-five cents in the country's wellbeing. Every citizen was issued a series of ration books for buying sugar, meat, cooking oil, and canned goods. I remember scrap drives to collect metal that could be used to build airplanes. We faced the possibility of being conquered by our enemies, and we avoided that outcome by collective action. We felt our unity.

I'm now writing at a time when the human need to belong is emerging in ways that are frighteningly divisive. Our identity as Americans has been hijacked, replaced by "Us" and "Them" camps that keep us from addressing the real problems we face—that must be solved together or not at all. I want to be clear, however, that the disconnectedness that concerns me runs deeper than current US politics. In recent centuries people who look like me and speak my language have gone into cultures where people knew themselves as part of each other and of nature, and in ways subtle and crude have corroded that intactness. But with proper atonement, we may be forgiven, for we knew not what we were doing. We of Northern European ancestry had our own intact cultures torn apart before the Western Middle Ages. We are the people author and culture activist Stephen Jenkinson calls orphans,[63] without connection to our ancestral families, homes, and lands of long-ago origin. If our people had remained whole, they might not have led the march into industrialization that is now destroying us. We of the present day might not have so easily been duped into seeking convenience for ourselves and our nearest kin, at the expense of the welfare of the rest of the world.

COMMUNAL CULTURES CAN TEACH US VILLAGE-MINDEDNESS

It is ironic that to learn how to strengthen bonds between humans and between humans and nature, it would now be wise to seek out members of the last remaining deeply communal cultures we've almost destroyed. Most prominently for US Americans this would be the original North Americans. Robin Wall Kimmerer, an enrolled member of the Citizen Potawatomi Nation, said in an interview, "I remember an elder once saying that we have protected our traditional knowledge against so many assaults and that one day the whole world would need it."[64] American Indian ways of being have survived an onslaught by Europeans that consciously aimed to destroy them. Thomas Berry writes, "From having been one of the freest peoples who ever lived, they have become one of the most confined, culturally as well as physically." He continues:

> *One resource from which American tribal peoples draw strength for cultural survival is their awareness of having won a moral victory of unique dimensions during the past five centuries. Many peoples have been besieged during the course of history, . . . but it would be difficult to find a people who over such a long period have undergone such destructive influences yet have survived and preserved their identity so firmly as the American Indian.*[65]

The Mayans, the original Guatemalans, have survived onslaught by the Spanish, followed by intervention by the US government and American corporations. Martín Prechtel was in Guatemala during the earthquake of February 4, 1976. Learning of the need for food in high villages where the one road of access had disappeared, he raised money for rice, beans, and transportation, and found help to prepare the food. After hours traversing hard terrain in an old pickup truck, his group was found by one villager and guided to Cuchumaquic where about

300 survivors of several villages had gathered. The guide explained that while some had been sent out to find water or food, it had been seven days since most had eaten. Clay utensils had been pulverized by the shock. They had nothing to cook in had there been food, nor anything that would hold water, had their stream not been buried under tons of dirt and rubble. Hearing the number, the rescuers realized they were bringing only a portion of what would be needed, since they had distributed food already to several villages lower down the mountain.

> *With supplies in such desperate scarcity, we neared this great crowd of starving families, fully expecting to be mobbed by a horde of hunger-crazed people, pushing us out of the way, while the strongest individuals elbowed and clubbed their way to get closer to the precious sustenance. . . . I'd seen tragic masses of waving, hunger-driven arms and bodies besieging vehicles and food deliveries in more citified areas, and in some cases seriously injuring or even killing one another or those handing out the food. All of us in the back of the truck concurred that we should all leap away from the bed and get as far away as we could if it came to that, and then wait until we could reclaim the truck and then return from where we had set out.*
>
> *But in that anxious moment of entering Cuchumaquic there were no desperate people running or a happily cheering crowd. . . . (When) we ground down into a gear-crunching halt right into the middle of hundreds of sitting people in some seventy family groups, comforting their wounded, broken, and dying, their half conscious babies and bewildered old folk lying inside the attentive circle of those who continued a little stronger, not one of the people stirred.*[66]

Prechtel made the invitational announcement, said a blessing over the rice and beans, and apologized for the inadequacy of the amount.

> *A momentary silence landed over our settling dust as everybody looked back at us with six hundred tired, sweet eyes. Then from every side, in an instant of parallel motion characteristic of a communal mind, an individual man or woman, representing their hungry families, their wounded, their young, their old, came gracefully to their feet, each man removing his hat if he*

still had one, the women with their hands waving to the rhythm of the poetry of their collective response.[67]

To die together had been their expectation, and as long as they were together, they were at peace. They experienced a depth of belonging, to each other and to the land, that was enough to carry them through the suffering caused by an earthquake that injured over 76,000 and claimed more than 22,700 lives.

We have come to the heart of the matter

For me to suggest that we aspire—and train—to experience a degree of this kind of belonging, so that we might be serene in the midst of a collapse as deadly as an earthquake, is perhaps not the expected message, and I feel hesitant about offering it. For more than twenty years I've been a climate activist, working to change the direction of society in order to prevent what I now hope to prepare us to endure. I still lend support to some of these efforts—the ones that don't aim to keep industrialism going—but I've turned my emphasis from prevention to long-term adaptation, especially in light of our present-day societal division. Perhaps if we focus on re-building ties with our neighbors while also building deeper ties with nature, there will be improvement also in support for communal climate action. Or perhaps we will only be laying a foundation our children and grandchildren will use to bring in a more wholesome society after we're gone.

Regardless of what else happens as a result of attention to our connections, however, we ourselves will be happier people. If we humbly seek to restore severed bonds and face the future holding hands, at least some of us will find the depth of belonging we haven't enjoyed, those of us of European ancestry, since the Romans invaded our lands, since formalized Christianity subsumed our sacred festivals, since both Catholics and Protestants burned alive our healers, since the Enclosures stole our livelihoods, since the Enlightenment blunted our sensitivities, and since neoliberal individualism shaped us into passive consumers.

As is probably true for you as well, I've done the best I knew to do regarding connection. Since childhood my heart has been tender toward living things, and my spiritual practice includes a lifestyle that is modest within the terms of this affluent culture. But I've been shaped by all the factors I've mentioned, and neither properly respecting nature nor thoroughly practicing community are things we can do successfully except within a community committed to a radically sharing, radically connected way of life.

This is what we pursue, and what we have to offer others: deeper connections. A realization of belonging is ahead for us if we take every step on the path to village-mindedness—magnified by the number of villagers we take into our hearts. This is "I'm well if you're well" when it includes everyone, human and more-than-human. The Bible calls it *agape*, and while we rarely rise to that capacity—to love anyone unconditionally, much less a village or a planet—the concept is the high mark on the wall, which signifies that if we grow that large, we'll know the sweetness Dante describes in *The Divine Comedy*:

> *The love of God, unutterable and perfect,*
> *flows into a pure soul the way that light*
> *rushes into a transparent object.*
> *The more love that it finds, the more it gives*
> *itself; so that, as we grow clear and open,*
> *the more complete the joy of heaven is.*
> *And the more souls who resonate together,*
> *the greater the intensity of their love,*
> *and, mirror-like, each soul reflects the other.*[68]

WE CAN UNDO THE CONDITIONING THAT KEEPS US IN SHALLOW RELATIONSHIPS

Alas, there are obstacles in the way as we reach toward that high mark, and some of those obstacles are likely to be ourselves. I may want to live in community, I may believe village-mindedness is the best way to view my neighbors, and yet my words and actions may make it hard for me to realize that goal. Wanting to play fair, trying not to ruffle feathers, and meeting the world with a smile are not enough. We are products of a culture that has not treated people well. We have good genes, but we carry wounds.

In *The Different Drum*, Scott Peck describes his experiences working with groups that wanted to come together in a closer way. He says that invariably they begin the workshop with the best of intentions. Participants greet each other, find subjects in common, and begin to get acquainted. But after this period, which he calls pseudo-community, they run into trouble. They encounter seemingly irreconcilable differences. They are not as happy, they don't know how to proceed, they may be sorry they came. He calls it the period of chaos—impasse. At that point he would tell them they were getting nowhere toward their goal of closeness. He would use the term emptiness for the state each would have to attain before the group could move together into real community. He writes, "I tell them simply that they need to empty themselves of barriers to communication. And I am able to use their behavior during chaos to point out to them specific things—feelings, assumptions, ideas, and motives—that have so filled their minds as to make them as impervious as billiard balls."[69]

The barriers to communication Peck mentions include:

Expectations and preconceptions: trying to fit others into a preconceived mold

Prejudices: judging people before we know them

Ideological or theological rigidity: feeling superior based on categories of belief

The need to heal, convert, fix, or solve: assuming that differences are unacceptable

The need to control: trying to insure the desired outcome.

Adulthood is not too late to become more open

The reason it is hard to change is that distancing habits are also defenses, and I believe we develop them only because at one time they were needed. A child comes into the world without affectations; they are acquired in order to manage real conditions. Once we become adults we need them in fewer situations, and yet they are not easily shed. Peck writes, "Giving them up is a sacrificial process. Consequently the stage of emptiness in community development is a time of sacrifice."

Childrearing practices that Americans consider appropriate, such as making behavioral demands, may nevertheless intimidate the developing human. We can contrast typical upbringing in our society with the reports of researchers studying contemporary hunter-gatherers' treatment of children. Ten different hunter-gatherer researchers responded to a questionnaire representing seven different hunter-gatherer cultures, and the picture was fairly uniform. Peter Gray writes, "Their treatment of children is very much in line with their treatment of adults. They do not use power-assertive methods to control behavior; they believe that each person's needs are equally important; and they believe that each person, regardless of age, knows best what his or her own needs are. Moreover, just as is the case with adults, children are not dependent on any specific other individuals, but upon the band as a whole, and this greatly reduces the opportunity for any specific individuals, including their parents, to dominate them."[70]

"We are sometimes told that children who are treated so kindly become spoiled," comments Elizabeth Marshall Thomas, "but this is because those who hold that opinion have no idea how successful such measures can be. Free from frustration or anxiety, sunny and cooperative, and usually without close siblings as competitors, the Ju/'hoan children were every parent's dream. No culture can ever have raised better, more intelligent, more likable, more confident children."[71] Raised in such an environment, a child doesn't need to develop such defenses, and would not need them as an adult in that same culture.

The goal is to relate to each other as human beings. The most helpful strategy I've found for moving in that direction is a communication method developed by Marshall Rosenberg. He calls it Nonviolent Communication or NVC, and says the goal is "to strengthen our ability to remain human, even under trying conditions. . . . All that has been integrated into NVC has been known for centuries. The intent is to remind us about what we already know—about how we humans were meant to relate to one another."[72]

Six years ago I joined an intentional community, and somewhat later a few of our members studied Rosenberg's book, *Nonviolent Communication*. In it he writes, "Long before I reached adulthood I learned to communicate in an impersonal way that did not require me to reveal what was going on inside myself." That is what was happening in the groups Scott Peck worked with. Participants were being impersonal, unrevealing, like mannequins or robots—or billiard balls, to use Peck's term. Rosenberg says, "I believe life-alienating communication is rooted in views of human nature that have exerted their influence for several centuries. These views stress humans' innate evil and deficiency."[73] We develop life-alienating habits due to the life-alienating philosophy of our culture.

We can learn life-supporting communication

To deepen our connections with others we need to learn life-supporting communication and behavior. The issues Rosenberg addresses are similar to the barriers Peck spotlights: moralistic judgments, making comparisons, denying responsibility, communicating our desires as commands. Rosenberg says these habits block compassion, which is our natural state when relating to others. We do this because we are not in touch with our feelings. Early in life, as a means of self-protection, we learned to cut ourselves off from what's going on inside ourselves. His practices are designed to help people recover their natural consideration for others by helping people become aware of their feelings. I will spotlight three features of the NVC method.

WE CAN OBSERVE WITHOUT EVALUATING

The first skill he suggests developing is "observe without evaluating." To achieve clear communication and thinking, I am to speak accurately, based on that moment's actual observation. "I observed that you . . ." Reality is ever changing. I may be tempted to make comparisons or generalize, perhaps remembering similar experiences. To do so removes the "clean slate" option that helps relationships move forward. I am to deal with one particular situation at a time, based on observation.

A similar standard appears in *The Dao de Jing* commentary by Ames and Hall—which validates Rosenberg's claim "all that has been integrated into NVC has been known for centuries." Ames and Hall write of the *wuwei* actions of the Dao master, "Actions uncompromised by stored knowledge or ingrained habits . . . are accommodating and spontaneous." Further, "It is not through an internal struggle of reason against the passions [this agrees with Rosenberg's counsel to honor feelings] but through 'acuity'—a mirroring of the things of the world as they are in their relationship to us [Rosenberg: observing]—that we reach a state in which nothing of all the myriad of the 'goings on' in the world will be able to agitate our hearts-and-minds, and we are able to promote the flourishing of our world."[74] If we approach each social transaction without bias or history hindering our power to observe, we not only allow the other person a fresh start, but we relieve ourselves of a burden and are "able to promote the flourishing of our world." This is how we deepen our connections. I help you and I help myself when I simply and with acuity *observe* the moment's event.

WE CAN LEARN: I OBSERVE, I FEEL, I NEED, AND I WANT

We are not, however, to ignore our own needs and we are not to be passive when they are not met. A second important suggestion from the Rosenberg method tells me how to approach a person when a transaction has troubled me. He says to begin by noticing my feelings and needs. If I recognize how I feel, I can ask for exactly what I need from the other person. Here is the sequence he recommends I use when I am disturbed by an interaction:

(1) I observe concrete actions that affect my wellbeing,
(2) I notice how I feel in relation to what I observe,
(3) I connect my feelings to the needs, values, or desires that create them, and
(4) I request concrete actions in order to enrich my life.[75]

Following these guidelines, he suggests a mother might say to her teenaged son, "Felix, I see three pairs of your soiled socks under the living room coffee table. When I see them I feel irritated, because I need more order in the rooms we share in common. Would you be willing to either put your socks in your room when you take them off or put them in the washing machine?" There is no judgment in the request, no generalization, no diagnosis, blame, insult, put-down, label, criticism, or comparison. There is only "I observe, I feel, I need, and I want."

Felix may agree or he may say he agrees and then forget about it, but he isn't likely to raise a big fuss, given the mother's respectful wording, at least in a home where respect has a strong history. The mother's tone was possible because she had dealt with her feelings of frustration or anger before stepping forward to make such a request. (Another Rosenberg theme is that we are responsible for our own feelings.) I find that identifying the unmet need and picturing myself speaking up about it gives that relief. I am calmed and can then be gracious in an eye-to-eye conversation that revisits the provocation. Will the four-point strategy always end satisfyingly? There's no guarantee, but this approach keeps the possibility of satisfaction alive.

WE CAN VIEW EVERY ACT AS AN ATTEMPT TO MEET NEEDS

The third suggested approach I want to spotlight is related. When I'm uncomfortable during an incident, Rosenberg suggests I look for the needs behind the other person's conduct or words, because every act is an attempt to meet needs. Thom Bond, a student of NVC, wrote a book about his experiences with the method. He tells a story about one of those Thanksgiving-visits-with-parents nightmares we've all had or heard about. His father began quizzing him about his current work project. They had been down that road many times, and Thom had always felt criticized. His chest began to tighten. The dialogue did follow the familiar pattern, since the dad asked the same kinds of questions to which the son could truthfully give only the same kinds of answers. But this time, applying his NVC training, Thom took stock, paused, and began following his father's words with a new kind of attention. He thought, "I have an unmet need here. I'm wanting to be seen. . . . What is my father's need?" He recited internally, "All acts are attempts to meet needs."

And then, at the point where his father voiced his judgmental conclusion about his son's approach to work, Thom said, "'So Dad, it sounds like you really want me to do well out there and you would love it if I could benefit from your experience. Is that true?' After some silence, in a tone that seemed a combination of relief and delight, his father said, 'Yes, yes it is.'" Thom wrote, "Right before my eyes he transformed from a 'critical, didactic know-it-all' to a man who loved his son and wanted to help him succeed."[76]

I note that Thom might have chosen to confront Dad's poor behavior with a request to change: "Would you be willing to listen to my point of view?" What he did was far better, though. He changed his own point of view. Based on what he observed, he gave his father a free pass, and both of them gained what they most needed: a closer relationship.

We can practice non-attachment

To those familiar with Buddhist principles, Rosenberg's counsel to see with an open mind should sound familiar. Therapist Rachel Gordon has written, "Acceptance, in Buddhist terms, refers to our ability to stay present. When life presents us with something the ego finds painful and not pleasurable, the mind's tendency is to resist, avoid, change or generally push against. . . . So in order to experience (and potentially change) anything, we are instructed to first 'say yes,' lean in and simply let go of the effort and energy we invest in resisting reality. The Buddha said that attachment (and its opposite, aversion) is the root of all suffering."[77]

> *Why dost thou strive and struggle, and day and night art full of concern?*
> *Be thou the same whatever betide, for what is, is; what is not, is not.*
> *Short is life, and many its troubles; why so anxious in your heart?*
> *Be thou satisfied with wet or dry, for what is, is; what is not, is not.*
>
> KHUSHAL KHAN KHATTAK,
> National Poet of Afghanistan[78]

To give up attachments doesn't mean to stifle feelings. It means to recognize emotions and the needs they spring from. When I have identified my true needs, with my adult power I can address them. With my neighbors I can be forthright without criticism stated or implied, and receive their requests in the same spirit.

To replace life-alienating patterns of communication, I've been trying to attend to what is. I try to observe, to apply my curiosity to the matter, to see with an open mind. The reward of accepting the existence of reality rather than spending energy resisting it is inner peace, and one of the rewards of inner peace is more tranquil relationships.

In summary, our culture has imposed many hindrances to deep connections, and one of the most serious is the envelope of acquired habits of thought and communication with which most of us surround ourselves beginning in childhood. To advise "Just be yourself" is to suggest the impossible, if I am shrouded in mystery even to my own mind. The distancing techniques that were successful in hiding me from critics when I was small can now be laid down. With the help of teachings like the ones I've mentioned we can communicate directly and without subterfuge. This is a big step, but with practice it will move us closer to our goal of stronger connections with others. The more genuine I become, the better friend and neighbor I can be.

WE CAN LEARN WHAT IT MEANS TO LIVE WITHIN COMMUNITY

Dmitri Orlov has written about societal collapse in Russia, and he anticipates systemic failure in the United States as well. He sees breakdown happening in five stages. First the financial sector crumbles, including banks; then the commercial sphere fails because business are unable to survive; then government services shut down one by one for lack of funding. In the fourth stage, he writes, "society fragments into extended families and small tribes of a dozen or so families, who find it advantageous to band together for mutual support and defense. This is the form of society that has existed over some 98.5% of humanity's existence as a biological species and can be said to be the bedrock of human existence. Humans can exist at this level of organization for thousands, perhaps millions of years." He says a locally based, gift-giving economy can keep life fairly comfortable as people lower their expectations. Stage Five, he says, doesn't have to ever happen, unless "pre-collapse society is too atomized, alienated and individualistic to form cohesive extended families and tribes."[79]

> Now, if you listen closely.
> I'll tell you what I know
> Storm clouds are gathering
> The wind is gonna blow
> The race of man is suffering
> And I can hear the moan,
> 'Cause nobody,
> But nobody
> Can make it out here alone.
>
> Alone, all alone
> Nobody, but nobody
> Can make it out here alone.
>
> MAYA ANGELOU[80]

Even within our current circumstances we should be able to form a mini-village — an alliance that has the potential to hang together through hard times. I expect if things start coming down all around and customary public services begin to fail, it will take a group of nearby others to help us meet our daily needs. In every neighborhood there are likely to be a few people willing to pool resources and look together for ways to deal with the worsening circumstances. We can prepare ourselves to become valuable members of such informal alignments. A group like this can be a realistic step toward avoiding social breakdown.

When one of my daughters and I moved into a small, multi-generational house in an intentional community, we saw this choice as a means to reduce our load on the planet. We both felt drawn to a less individualistic way of life and wanted to deepen our commitment to a low-consumption lifestyle. I also viewed it as a personal benefit, one that would enable me to continue gardening as I grew older, for example. I thought it was wise to provide myself with neighbors who would care about me as a matter of course, rather than relying on compatibility or luck.

I see it now as a societal contribution. Some have criticized intentional community ventures as retreating from the world, but my experience is otherwise. As our members create an alliance that gives each one a network of supporters, we are pro-actively engaged in resisting individualistic forces. We are learning skills that will be useful in our small town and county.

But community can be built in any location. If I had stayed in my single-family suburban house, I would try to do the same thing there. If my unintentional neighbors and I, who just happened to live near each other — if we chose to do what most needs to be done, we'd be building bridges of connection to serve our very human need to belong.

> *This is a truth as old as the hills. Our distant ancestors knew the importance of the collective and rarely idolized individuals. Perhaps they understood the human condition better than we do today.*
>
> JEREMY LENT[81]

> *Is it any wonder then, that loneliness can quite literally make us sick? ... Human beings crave togetherness and interaction. Our spirits yearn for connection just as our bodies hunger for food.*
>
> RUTGER BREGMAN[82]

Building connections is the work of our time. Unfortunately we may lack the skills that would enable us to accomplish it with the people we find ourselves tied to when chaos hits. In countries where people are primarily seen as individuals rather than as members of a community, we may grow from childhood into adults with successful careers and families and yet not know how to function in a co-operative way. The word co-operate in our culture is often used as a synonym for conform. "Co-operate, folks" can mean we are expected to co-operate with a leader on a plan handed down to us from above.

To co-operate is to operate with equal authority

The spelling I'm using here shows the more accurate meaning of the word. When we "co"-operate, we're members of a team on which everyone has equal authority. To co-operate is be partners in operating. When you and I co-operate, we have roles that correspond in significance though they may not be identical.

Egalitarian rather than elite-led or hierarchic power arrangements are more effective in the long run. When I joined the intentional community, I came in with traditional ideas about organizational structure: distribute the necessary leading roles as fairly as possible, specify the task assignments for each role, and encourage leaders and followers to be kind to each other. To my surprise and with my disapproval, there arose resistance to any sign of leadership; to me it seemed petty to be unwilling to let others have higher status even for a term of office. It seemed excessive to want to remove rank altogether, and I expected inefficiency and many long delays to follow.

I was right about the delays; group decision-making takes more time than top-down management. I believe I was mistaken, however, about the inefficiency. To evaluate the effectiveness of a course of action we must look at the long-term results as well as the early steps. If the outcome proves more satisfying because its benefits reach a wider circle and are more enduring, the time has been well spent.

The boys show us how it's done

Rutger Bregman's book *Humankind: A Hopeful History* increases my confidence in the co-operative possibilities. Bregman is not an anthropologist examining artifacts to determine Iron Age characteristics or living with the last few surviving hunter-gatherers. He is a twenty-something European writer re-examining incidents that took place in recent decades. He is asking whether modern humans are still cooperative and altruistic. He delves into newspaper archives, libraries, and internet searches, and with the help of energetic reporters who share his skepticism about standard versions of popular stories, he has discovered that some tales that have become almost mythic in their import have in fact been wrong.

He questioned the assumption that savagery such as occurred in *Lord of the Flies* by William Golding would be a typical outcome in the case of schoolboys finding themselves alone on a remote island. After a great deal of searching, he came across a real-life account of boys who had been stranded on an island. He located the man who had rescued them, and also one of the survivors. The true story is very different from the one in Golding's tale.

In June of 1965 six boys, pupils at St. Andrews boarding school in the Tongan capitol of Nuku'alofa, ran away in a stolen fishing boat, taking with them as supplies only two sacks of bananas, several coconuts, and a small gas burner. None of the boys, ages thirteen to sixteen, knew anything about sailing, and they took no compass or map. On the first night a storm tore up the sail and the rudder, and they drifted for eight days, with each having a sip twice each day of rainwater collected in a coconut shell.

On the ninth day they came to Ata, an uninhabited rock many miles from Tonga. When one of the boys succeeded in producing a spark by rubbing sticks together, they kept the fire going for more than a year. They divided the work of survival and handled arguments with timeouts followed by apologies. They began and ended each day with a song and a prayer. When they were rescued in September of 1966, all were in perfect physical condition, even a boy who had fallen and broken his leg.[83]

These children spent sixteen months together and bonded in an orderly, life-saving community before they were rescued. With only the guidance of their genetic inheritance: egoism, nepotism, and an altruism that had been strengthened by moral codes learned from family and school, they created a six-member youth village that enabled them to do more than merely survive. The task at which they succeeded is something like what I expect our mini-villages will be called on to do.

Community is hindered by our language

A friend from Senegal told me that in his village, if there is a fire, every member grabs a bucket, fills it with water, and hurries to put out the flames. If a person doesn't join the rescue effort, not only that person but every member of that person's generation must make amends to all the rest of the village. The entire community experiences both the shame of having withheld help and the benefit of the compensation.

This kind of communality is almost unthinkable in our setting, in which we aim to make individuals pay for their offenses without reference to the social structures that may have shaped their behavior. Our legal system and even our language points us toward individualism and distancing. Languages both reflect and then further determine the values of their speakers, and English speakers who want to change culture often find vocabulary lacking. In recent decades this problem has been addressed in several ways that may be helpful as we pursue communality.

Martin Buber added a phrase when his book *I and Thou* was translated from German into English in 1937.[84] He proposed using "thou," the intimate form of the second person pronoun "you" as a signal that I honor the worth of the person with whom I am relating. As a child raised on the King James Bible who had also studied Spanish, it was natural for me to understand what he meant. But other English speakers may need to be told that most languages have one "you," that could be translated as "thou," to indicate familiarity, endearment, or intimacy, and they also have a different, formal word for "you" that they use with strangers for professional exchanges. In English since the 1700s, "you" is always impersonal; we've lost our "thou."

Even our language pushes us away from the connectedness available to other cultures. While it may be impractical to begin saying "thou" in all circumstances that apply, I do find it helpful in my thinking. It's also interesting that the English translation of Buber's text includes this sentence: "The basic word I-You (Thou) can only be spoken with one's whole being." The basic word I-It can never be spoken with one's whole being. We can easily understand the difference between a "you" and an "it."

And that is the point Robin Wall Kimmerer wants to make when she says, "In Anishinaabe and many other indigenous languages, it's impossible to speak of Sugar Maple as 'it.' Objectification of the natural world reinforces the notion that our species is somehow more deserving of the gifts of the world than the other 8.7 million species with whom we share the planet. Using 'it' absolves us of moral responsibility and opens the door to exploitation. When Sugar Maple is an 'it' we give ourselves permission to pick up the saw. Among the many examples of linguistic imperialism, perhaps none is more pernicious than the replacement of the language of nature as subject with the language of nature as object."

Kimmerer says we need a language "with its roots in an ancient way of thinking." She suggests new English pronouns for speaking of the more-than-human community: 'ki' with a plural 'kin.' "Look at that tree. Ki is so beautiful," and "See, kin are flying north for the winter."[85]

Thich Nhat Hanh has added a verb to the language with his term 'interbeing.' He writes, "'Interbeing' is a word that is not in the dictionary yet, but if we combine the prefix 'inter-' with the verb 'to be,' we have a new verb, inter-be." He explains, "Without a cloud, there will be no rain; without rain, the trees cannot grow; and without trees, we cannot make paper. The cloud is essential for the paper to exist. If the cloud is not here, the sheet of paper cannot be here either. So we can say that the cloud and the paper inter-are."[86]

When I began writing on these topics many years ago, I was irritated to find we have no word for life without violence. It may be accurate to characterize the boys in *Lord of the Flies* as "violent," but "non-violent" doesn't begin to describe the way of life the six Tongan boys created on that uninhabited rock in the middle of the ocean. "Peaceful" describes only one aspect of the boys' community, as do "orderly" or "pleasing" or "compassionate"—all substitutes we might apply. Marshall Rosenberg chose to call his communication method non-violent for lack of that missing positive English word. In this writing, to name the conditions under which we would live together supportively, I'm saying "village-mindedness" or "communality." That our English-speaking forbears had little knowledge of the condition we are forced to call non-violent is a fair conclusion to be drawn. It falls to us to create the condition and at the same time find words to name it.

We can take small steps toward community

Perhaps the ordinary rituals of personal relationships are the place to begin in order to make community seem more realizable. My friend Pete calls it the art of being friendly. He says befriending begins with the simple skills of reciprocal conversation. You start by asking about how the person or family is doing. "You feel genuine interest that opens the way to take it to the next level, where you find commonalities." For daily exercise he walks around a neighborhood lake, and he said, "Of the people I often walk around the lake with, three or four have real difficulty talking about something other than themselves and their particular subject, but yet we are friends. We first learn to listen really well, hear the feelings, and find each other's common values and interests and enjoy each other's company."

And even chance greetings of strangers can help us to feel less alone.

> I've been thinking about the way, when you walk
> down a crowded aisle, people pull in their legs
> to let you by. Or how strangers still say "bless you"
> when someone sneezes, a leftover
> from the Bubonic plague. "Don't die," we are saying.
> We have so little of each other, now. So far
> from tribe and fire. Only these brief moments of exchange.
> What if they are the true dwelling of the holy, these
> fleeting temples we make together when we say, "Here,
> have my seat," "Go ahead—you first," "I like your hat."
>
> DANUSHA LAMÉRIS[87]

With a little more time, such gestures of solidarity can be nurtured into friendships, and even casual acquaintances relieve the isolation that is a threat to wellbeing. Building bridges between ourselves and others is crucial to our security even now, when most of us are still living in relative comfort and safety, physically speaking. We can't connect with everyone we pass or speak with, but it has never been more important to be aware of their presence with us in the world, and to make time to go deeper when there is opportunity.

Forming an "I've got your back" group is very much like befriending one person. It will take a bit more time and more tact, because each of the individuals will have a different perspective, to which we will want to pay attention. We are offering something everyone needs—belonging and help—and we're asking them to share an obligation. We do this with an optimistic attitude, because our neighbors are human, they share our need and our genetic evolution, and to a large extent they share our enculturation. A closer look at gathering a group that will help each other manage the difficulties can be found in Appendix II: Forming a Mini-Village.

Indigenous thinking doesn't have to be learned only from people who've preserved their ancient ways. We too can be authentic. To come alive and become more human, all we have to do is be awake: hear, see, smell—use our senses to observe and our minds and hearts to appreciate other beings. We can recognize and value each other, and value every square foot of the ground we occupy. Each element weighs into the whole—here comes into play a caution Marshall Rosenberg gives about comparison, and the Dao de Jing's ideal of resisting stored knowledge or ingrained habits. Worth is not measurable unless we monetize each other or apply a false utilitarian assessment. Every square foot of grass is filled with life, none more or less valuable than every human. Worth is a feature of being.

I believe we can include in our village even people who don't share the extent of our altruism, because many of them, despite their bias against inclusiveness, are committed to being honest and reliable. What we can hope for is that our kindness and friendship and our model of reciprocal sharing will gain value in the eyes of people who come toward us initially with narrow sympathies. I've seen friendships develop between people who hold such opposing views, and I've experienced it. "Love drew a circle big enough" is our mark on the wall. The closer we get to it, the sweeter life is.

I must say here that to draw the circle big enough to include everyone may be a superhuman posture, a stance a person cannot achieve without spiritual help. In the first handbook I related how the eternal verities such as love, generosity, and forgiveness have guided me, and I hope I made clear that I experience them as agents of change. They have the power to move me into attitudes and behaviors beyond my ordinary inclinations. They prompt me, and when I follow, they unite my heart with their purposes so that I am more open and caring. Through what feels to me like a personal intervention, they shape me until my sympathies are expansive—in the image of God, as it says in the book of Genesis. (Gen 1:27 KJV).

Your particular spiritual helpers have the power to move you out of the shell our cultural setting virtually demanded of most of us in formative years. You are bigger than you know, with a softer outline. Every human has the potential to develop more caring capacity, and if we are to build community amid the turmoil of these years, we will need to make fuller use of our spiritual as well as our social assets.

I can search among my neighbors, choose the one I least understand or even least admire, and if I create a scenario in which we two are the last people alive in this part of the world, I can discover that this person would be a good partner if she is willing. We could help and enjoy each other, and it would not be because each of us filled a function or role. It is because, in our natures, we are complex and fascinating. We are of great worth.

And what is all this worth and value for? I don't think the best use of humans is drudgery in a factory—or in an office or classroom. The best use of mountains is not to be scraped for coal. The purpose of all of this amazing life must be like the purpose of a star, meant for wonder and joy. So while we grieve our losses, as people and trees die and the grass dries up from drought or burns away in fire, doesn't every remaining fragment of this world become more precious, including its humans?

In my view the restoration of deep connections could make it possible to resolve our problems short of collapse.

- If we can realize our unity with all other humans and with more-than-human nature, then humans can band together to address the suffering in the human world.
- If this change of understanding can take place quickly enough, we might band together to reduce our consumption of Earth resources and stop making waste, so that Earth can continue to sustain her various life forms.
- Our need to deepen our connections with other humans will dramatically increase as the consequences of the destructive economy come down upon us.
- The need to deepen our connections with the more-than-human world will also increase, as Earth's ability to sustain her life forms diminishes. Scarcity will increase our appreciation of whatever support Earth can continue to give.
- And even if we don't act in time to avoid the collapse of the order we've had until now, the restoration of deep connections might be the means of human survival.

IN CONCLUSION

When Martín Prechtel encountered the quiet crowd at Cuchumaquic, he noticed a man who seemed to bear a great deal of responsibility and be held in an unusual degree of respect for one so young. The man sheltered under his arm a pouch that was clearly special—decorated as if ceremonially significant. When they conversed during the meal (of which Prechtel and all the younger village men for the sake of kindness only pretended to partake) the man disclosed the contents: two perfect ears of heritage corn. Under no circumstances would any of those people have considered eating that corn. Not to avoid starvation and their own extinction. It was their legacy, their village wealth, and it was meant to save lives in some future village, after all of them had passed away.[88]

If all we can reasonably expect to accomplish, given the extent of the harm at the time our leaders take appropriate action, is to make a good effort toward some future world that we will not live to see, this is the way we would do it: by deepening our connections.

What I'm seeking is to take us back to the most fundamental aspects of being human. On an individual level, people often get there through serious illness or a devastating loss. A bonding event that brings a majority collectively to our knees may be required, and who can say that this will not happen? As the present social and economic systems break down and we face basic problems of survival, like the need for food and water and the necessity of cooperating with neighbors to obtain them, we may look at the world with fresh eyes. I would prefer that we recover wisdom in time to avoid the worst outcomes, but whether humans make the shift early or late in the inevitable transition from this particular form of civilization, I hope we make it. Human beings are amazing creatures, well worth a new chance at life.

Whenever I doubt the character of the human species, I start naming the fine humans I know or have read about. Here I share a few final quotations from people whose work or words I value.

> *Now you are responsible for the safety of this overbearing dome as much as you are for your own health and wealth. It weighs on you, body and soul. To survive under these new conditions we have to undergo a sort of metamorphosis.*
>
> BRUNO LATOUR, philosopher, anthropologist, and author of *After Lockdown: A Metamorphosis*[89]

> *And that's the question, what can I really change after all, and first of all, I can change myself, not necessarily the basic architecture of my personality, but I can change my attitudes,*

I can change my behavior, I can change my shallow but angry thinking, and I can think more critically, read more widely, gain more compassion. And without the anger, I might be able to affect more than I can with it.

> VICKI ROBIN, Social innovator, writer, speaker, and co-author of Your Money or Your Life[90]

After the distancing a new intimacy; after the mechanistic a greater biological sensitivity; after damaging a healing. We need only look at the surrounding universe in its more opaque material aspects—look at it, listen to it, feel and experience the full depths of its being. Suddenly its opaque quality, its resistance, falls away, and we enter into a world of mystery. What seemed so opaque and impenetrable becomes radiant with intelligibility.

> THOMAS BERRY, Passionist priest, cultural historian, and author[91]

We can succeed only by concert. It is not "can any of us imagine better?" but, "can we all do better?" The dogmas of the quiet past are inadequate to the stormy present. The occasion is piled high with difficulty, and we must rise—with the occasion. As our case is new, so we must think anew, and act anew. We must disenthrall ourselves, and then we shall save our country.

Fellow-citizens, we cannot escape history. We of this Congress and this administration, will be remembered in spite of ourselves. No personal significance, or insignificance, can spare one or another of us. The fiery trial through which we pass, will light us down, in honor or dishonor, to the latest generation.

> ABRAHAM LINCOLN, December 1, 1862[92]

Life is about more than survival. We are all more likely to engage willingly in the collective effort described above if we are able to enjoy ourselves in the process. Over the next few decades, we need to build a social system that differs radically from the industrial, consumption-oriented, growth economy of

the 20th century. Let's make it a beautiful human world, filled
with opportunities for singing, dancing, reflecting, remembering,
imagining, mourning, meditating, and all the other life-
sustaining activities that go on in a healthy culture.

>RICHARD HEINBERG, Journalist, Senior Fellow-in-Residence of the Post Carbon Institute, author of thirteen books[93]

> I sometimes forget
> that I was created for Joy.
> My mind is too busy
> My heart is too heavy
> for me to remember
> that I have been
> called to dance
> the sacred dance of life.
> I was created to smile
> To Love
> To be lifted up
> And to lift others up.

>HAFEZ, fourteenth-century Persian lyric poet[94]

When a friend calls to me from the road
And slows his horse to a meaning walk,
I don't stand still and look around
On all the hills I haven't hoed,
And shout from where I am, What is it?
No, not as there is a time to talk.
I thrust my hoe in the mellow ground,
Blade-end up and five feet tall,
And plod: I go up to the stone wall
For a friendly visit.

>ROBERT FROST, American poet[95]

HANDBOOK THREE
Acquiring Useful Knowledge

Handbook Three
ACQUIRING USEFUL KNOWLEDGE

Contents

Adaptation will likely involve a lot more self-provisioning / 89
Self-provisioning is not a totally foreign way of life / 91
Industrial culture has made self-provisioning seem abnormal / 96

WHERE WILL OUR FOOD COME FROM? / 100

Preparing permanent beds / 102
Selecting important vegetables / 105
    SWISS CHARD / 106
    IRISH POTATOES / 107
    SOUTHERN COWPEAS / 108
    SWEET POTATOES / 108
    ONIONS AND GARLIC / 109
Caring for garden vegetable plants / 111
Additional resources / 115

HOW WILL WE MEET OUR NEED FOR CLEAN WATER? / 117

Community water systems now face significant problems / 118
Groundwater may become our direct source of water / 118
Water purification will be an important skill to acquire / 121
    CARBON FILTERS / 121
    BIOSAND FILTRATION / 123
    UV-A LIGHT DISINFECTION / 125
Water storage may enable us to stay where we are / 126
    CISTERNS / 126
    RAIN BARRELS / 127
    STORING WATER IN THE LAND, BERMS AND SWALES / 128
    STORING WATER IN THE LAND, KEYLINE / 130
Water conservation plays a large role in water provisioning / 132
Additional resources / 135

HOW WILL WE PROVIDE FOR SAFE SANITATION? / 135

Managing septic tanks / 137
Composting human excrement / 138
    THE FOUR BASIC REQUIREMENTS: #1 THE COVER MATERIAL / 139
    THE FOUR BASIC REQUIREMENTS: #2 THE COMPOST TOILET / 140
    THE FOUR BASIC REQUIREMENTS: #3 THE COMPOST BINS / 140

  THE FOUR BASIC REQUIREMENTS: #4 HUMAN MANAGEMENT / 142
  QUESTION #1 WHAT CAN BE COMPOSTED? / 142
  QUESTION #2 WHAT KIND OF PILE? / 142
  QUESTION #3 HOW MOIST DOES THE PILE NEED TO BE KEPT? / 143
  QUESTION #4 HOW IS THE PILE AERATED? / 143
  QUESTION #5 DOES THE PILE NEED TO BE TURNED? / 143
  QUESTION #6 IS IT LEGAL? / 144
  QUESTION #7 HOW SAFE IS THE COMPOST FROM A PROPERLY MANAGED COMPOST TOILET SYSTEM? / 144
  A HUMANURE TESTIMONY / 145

How will we dispose of potentially dangerous trash
  "COMPOST EVERYTHING" / 146
  NON-BIODEGRADABLE WASTE / 147

How will we keep clean in post-industrial conditions? / 148

OTHER RESOURCES / 152

AS WE TRANSITION TO A LESS DESTRUCTIVE WAY OF LIFE, WE MAY LEARN HOW TO PRODUCE RATHER THAN CONSUME, AND WE MAY COME TO VALUE EARTH'S WAYS MORE THAN THE WAYS OF OUR CULTURE.

We are in the teeth of a King Grizzly discontinuity, and it's shaking our material certainties and our cultural assumptions apart like a salmon-wrapped ragdoll. Oily stuffing is already flying in all directions.

ALEX STEFFEN[96]

Wealthy individuals and concerned businesses are preparing to protect themselves from climate change and any new health emergency by tapping an increasingly bespoke range of personal services and snapping up private hideaways that are out of reach for ordinary citizens.

HANNAH KUCHLER[97]

The modern world has overshot the limits of what the Earth can bear, and our civilization will collapse. The crucial questions now are (1) how much will be left, and (2) can we build something more sustainable in the ruins?

JOHN B. COBB, JR.[98]

The tensions of our day describe a civilization in the throes of momentous change. But whatever happens at the macro level, we do have power within our personal lives. To the extent of our power, we must use it well. We must apply ourselves to build up the resources at our command, for the present moment and for the future we cannot predict.

Here our focus is on the hidden asset of knowledge, the kind we carry in our heads and muscles as we move beyond "the age of information." Aleksandr Solzhenitsyn once wrote from prison, "Own only what you can always carry with you: know languages, know countries, know people. Let your memory be your travel bag. Use your memory! Use your memory! It is those bitter seeds alone which might sprout and grow someday."[99]

For many reasons, the Internet and other tools of prosperity technology—think smart phones, computers, and cable, or even daily print newspaper—may become less reliably at hand for reference. For the young who have always had a second "mind" at their fingertips and for older people whose minds are too full or faded to retrieve knowledge that was once mastered, this may be a serious loss. It will be for me. Yet even people my age can begin to use our minds more narrowly in order to focus on absorbing and retaining essential knowledge rather than trivia, and the minds of the young are in the period when the prefrontal cortex is most capable of acquiring new skills.

"We don't know where we're going, we don't know what's going to happen, just remember, no one can take away from you what you put in your mind."[100] These are the words the mother of holocaust survivor Dr. Edith Eger said to her daughters at the entrance to the Nazi prison camp in the moments before they were forever separated. Even if our situation is less dire, I think the reminder is helpful to us. We don't know what will happen tomorrow, but we have the chance today to prepare for whatever tomorrow may bring. I offer this handbook because I think increasing our store of practical knowledge ranks just behind strengthening our spirits and making deep connections with others as the most important preparation we can make.

What should we be learning in preparation for the changes we may face? This handbook will offer detailed information about three fundamental life skills that people in highly industrialized settings may know little about: food, water, and sanitation. I want to offer more than how-to-do-it information, however, because I see the period of crisis as a chance to build a better future. It can be a transition to a way of life that will be less destructive and more compatible with real human needs.

1. We may learn how to produce rather than consume.

2. We may come to value Earth's ways more than the ways of our culture.

I fear many people are leaning away from me at this point, hoping I won't say, "Learn to grow your own food." In fact I will make that suggestion, but food growing must now be viewed as one part of a major lifestyle modification, and it will be a lot more pleasurable to do it when the garden doesn't have to be wedged between all the social and economic expectations in today's schedules. I believe any mandatory letting go of current burdens offers an exchange that may be surprisingly attractive, once we have time to re-evaluate. The disruptions are giving us the chance to create a way of life that, while it may not be easier, may be far more satisfying than the one we will be leaving behind.

Adaptation will likely involve a lot more self-provisioning

I think we are moving toward an economy in which people will meet their needs by producing for themselves and near neighbors what is needed, whether it is essentials such as food and shelter, or pleasures like music and sports. For almost two centuries we've been encouraged to move production out of the home or neighborhood—and indeed the country—and by this date an American could dress in, travel by, and dine on goods made on other side of the world for long periods of time. We live in a consumer culture. Our culture consumes. That's what it does.

Although the future may not be entirely a "world made by hand," the title of a novel by James Howard Kunstler that describes a community trying to survive following national collapse, we may find it possible to make many of the things we now purchase. Before things settle into a new, more stable, sustainable economy, I think most of us may keep gardens and small animals for food; obtain and purify drinking water; and dispose of our own waste, primarily on the land where we live. We will need to know how to keep warm in winter and cool in summer, and how to cook our food and preserve our foodstocks. I think we or our neighbors may build, repair, and clean our homes; maintain whatever form of transportation we can manage to obtain; swap, mend, knit, and sew our clothing; nurse the sick, mentally ill, injured, and dying; and manage births and deaths including some form of burial. I expect we may have final responsibility for the mentally ill, the misfits, and the somewhat disorderly folks who are our kin or neighbors.

You may already do some of the things mentioned on one of these lists. Many people do, either by choice or necessity. Like me, they may have grown up when maintenance of house and car were household routines for their parents. Their mothers may have canned or frozen surplus vegetables and made jellies and preserves; their fathers may have changed the oil and performed other regular maintenance of the family car and lawnmower. And people without money have always managed to live without paid services, though not always well, as health statistics reveal.

When Mark Boyle decided to move out of the technological economy in 2013, he wrote that he did it out of "the burning desire to discover what it might feel like to become a part of one's landscape, using only tools and technologies (if I must call them that) which, like the Old Order Amish people of North America, do not make me beholden to institutions and forces that have no regard for the principles and values on which I wish to live my life." As a result of his decision, he learned the following skills: starting a fire without matches, sharpening tools, butchering a road-killed deer, making a candle, making quill and paints from nature, washing clothes without electricity or running water, dressing a deerskin, making a hot bath.[101]

The principles and values on which Boyle wished to live his life are similar to the values I believe our future offers if we approach it prepared: we can produce rather than consume, and we can come to value the ways of Earth more than the ways of our culture.

In my view our opportunity now is to reorganize our lives to center around meeting our true needs and those of our neighbors with our own strength and will. There are less exploitative ways to do most of the daily tasks that make our lives comfortable. We can learn them, as thinkers and planners have been urging us to do since the 1970s, when the most visible threat to industrial progress was peak oil.

John Michael Greer captures the enthusiasm of the visionaries of those days: "In the world of the twenty-first century, appropriate-tech mavens argued, the chief abundant energy and resources that supported the extravagant machinery of twentieth-century industrial nations would inevitably run short. Before that happened, a new breed of technology had to be invented and put into production. The new technologies they hoped to pioneer would use energy and resources sparingly; they would work with the cycles of nature rather than against them; they would meet human needs without placing unsustainable burdens on the biosphere. All over the world in those days, you could find little non-profits on shoestring budgets and small companies run by basement entrepreneurs hard at work making that dream a reality."[102]

These people hoped to create the means to move smoothly from industrialization into ecological civilization. They envisioned a world that, while it was marked by observing limits, could power the essential aspects of modern life. I'm looking at a 1975 compilation of such projects now: a book in which twelve pioneers describe their own designs for small-scale energy systems to use sun, wind, water, methane gas, and wood to produce energy to power the home.[103] I was part of that movement, though as an adopter, not an inventor. My library was filled with books on passive solar construction, organic farming and gardening, and manual tools such as a bicycle-pedaled water pump and the "two-woman saw."

Fifty years ago there was time to think big about new technologies. I believe we have lost most of that opportunity. We have not yet lost the ability to examine our situation, however, and we can invent new patterns that will make our lives more tranquil as now-common amenities disappear. The primary power we now have, as I've said, is in our own hands. We can move from being consumers toward becoming producers, and we can work in partnership with nature rather than in the mode of exploitation.

Self-provisioning is not a totally foreign way of life

For most of us the needed patterns will be new, but in North America we have intact non-Indigenous communities that never abandoned the old ways. Mark Boyle mentioned the Old Order Amish people as patterns for the life he wanted to live, one that was not beholden to institutions whose aims he opposed. As of 2021, over 350,000 Old Order Amish lived in the United States, many in Lancaster County, Pennsylvania. "The Amish are known for simple living, plain dress, Christian pacifism, and slowness to adopt many conveniences of modern technology, with a view neither to interrupt family time, nor replace face-to-face conversations whenever possible, and a view to maintain self-sufficiency. The Amish value rural life, manual labor, humility, and *Gelassenheit* (serenity)."[104]

For at least twenty years a Pennsylvania Amish family farm has been the source of most of the food I eat that is not grown in my garden or orchard. The people who own it have been guided by their religious and cultural values as they provided non-industrial organic meat and milk for customers who reject the altered foodstuffs of modern, federally favored agriculture. Along with some of their neighbors, they have contributed to the good health of many families outside their geographic area, shipping orders monthly for members of their buying club to pickup locations in other states. Their work has not been easy. In addition to the frustrations most owners of small farms in the United States experience due to government policy famously described as "get big or get out," these Amish have been targeted for their independence—they have dared to resist what they and their customers see as regulations that add harmful ingredients and processes to naturally wholesome foods.

They don't use internet. Customers communicate with them by phone and fax, the latter not sent to the farm directly. When I want to speak with them, I call. They observe religious holidays regardless of whether income might be lost. Their monthly letter is optimistic about the challenges and full of gratitude for the blessings. I doubt they will be able to continue the distance-selling part of their livelihood as transportation becomes too expensive, but their way of life, free as it is from dependence on the industrial economy, will continue. Daily they demonstrate that life without luxuries can be rich amid hard work and many hindrances.

> *While there is no way forward without vision, vision is not enough. We must apply our own labor to build that vision now, regardless of how "un-realistic" or "impractical" we are told it is. If we put our work only into opposing what we don't want, we build not love for our vision, but only longing. The first rule of ecological restoration is the restoration of our own labor. Human labor is the precious natural resource, concentrated, controlled and exploited, that has been wielded like a chainsaw against the rest of the natural world. Because of this, we must take it back from the chains of the market and restore it to the web of life.*
>
> MOVEMENT GENERATION JUSTICE AND ECOLOGY PROJECT[105]

To me there is joy when I take hold of a thing that has had a hold on me. When I change from passive acceptance of something less than good, and take charge by either molding it to fit, or leaving it behind, I am empowered. It is the difference between being a tool and being the one handling a tool. Of course I'm not free to use any tool in ways that violate nature's ways. Going forward, my power will depend on partnering with nature, ultimately the agent with power on this interconnected planet.

Our power over circumstances will increasingly be within the circle of home and bioregion, and although I'm still concerned about what's happening with the nation, my focus is increasingly on my home ground. It is here that I have agency and power—even political power. "It is often forgotten that . . . agency is a central political category and that at the heart of authoritarianism is an uninformed and often isolated and depoliticized subject who has relinquished their agency to the cult of the strongman."[106] People who have routinely gathered knowledge, have built relationships with people they can depend on, and are sturdy within their own spirits are not likely to relinquish their agency to anyone.

But maybe the power I can get excited about, exercised within the sphere of the household, is unappealing or unfamiliar to many readers. I view it as an advantage of my age that I know a lot about the pleasures of a self-provisioning way of life.

I was born in 1936 in a rural county in East Texas. During my early years, the place where my paternal grandparents lived was a small, income-producing, self-sustaining cotton farm. These people lived as their parents had done; they had few of the services and conveniences of our present society. They never owned a car. They kept mules, mostly for plowing, but also for pulling an open-bed, prairie-schooner-style 4'x 8' box wagon with one foot-high side panels.

Their house was built in pioneer Texas "dogtrot" style, with a breezeway front-to-back down the center, and a door or a window opening onto it from every room. With tall ceilings throughout, the plan provided summer cooling in that warm climate. Behind the kitchen was a screened porch with an opening in each direction. Opposite the kitchen was the windowless smokehouse, which always smelled like cured ham and bacon. The door on the east end of the porch led to the large vegetable garden. The one on the west opened into the back yard, where the barnyard was on the other side of the west fence. The pit-type outhouse was behind the main house.

A handmade wood stile—a ladder built into the fence—was the pedestrian gate between the yard and the barnyard to the west of the house. Their hand-drawn well was near the stile. Beyond the well toward the road was the chicken coop, with egg boxes reachable from outside the building, once I was tall enough. In my earliest years there was a heavy

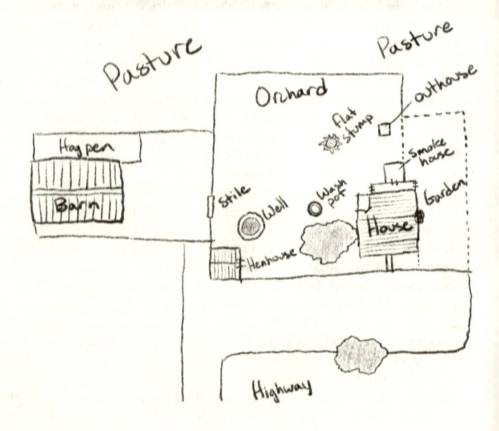

iron cauldron nearby for washing clothes, set over a fire pit and blackened by flames. Near the back porch was a wide, low stump where logs were split and chickens were slaughtered. The back part of the yard merged with the peach orchard, where six or seven large peach trees dependably bore fruit. In season we ate peaches under those trees, juice dripping onto our chins and shirts.

When we drew water from the well, we carried the bucket to the back porch, set it on the counter, and put a metal dipper into the pail for everyone to drink from. Water drunk from that dipper was cool and sweet; I thought it was the sweetest water in the world.

The counter was also the handwashing station. A happy snapshot in my mind is of handsome boy cousins washing up on the porch after helping Granddaddy in the fields. Stripped to the waist, their tanned shoulders bulging with young muscles, they poured water into a basin and splashed it on each other and slicked down wet hair as if getting ready for a Saturday night party. I wasn't privy to their plans; I was an admiring shadow pecking from behind the kitchen door. When they were through washing up, they pitched the remaining water out the door onto the garden.

I don't expect us to go back to that way of living, but there was much to love in those customs and places. Seen through my child eyes they were charming, and as I look back, I'm impressed by the knowledge base that kept this farm running. They knew how to plow a field with mules; raise cotton and get it to market; drive a wagon; care for cows, mules, hogs, and chickens; slaughter hogs and poultry; preserve pork without electricity; grow vegetables; maintain a well; build outbuildings and a stile; maintain an outhouse; do laundry outdoors over a fire; plant and tend an orchard, and keep a house cool in the sweltering East Texas heat. I would score low on a test of most of this knowledge, but at least I've seen it demonstrated.

It should be said that my grandparents were White landowners, not prosperous but without debt, with plenty of help from ten children and many grandchildren, most of whom stayed within twenty miles of their farm during those years. If they suffered hardship during the Great Depression, I never heard it mentioned, except that Grandmother never forgave Henry Wallace (Secretary of Agriculture in 1933) for making them butcher pigs as part of a government effort to raise prices on agricultural products. There was far more suffering for Black people in the same area, and for landless Whites or anyone in Southern cities. My good fortune didn't blind me to other people's poverty, but it did give me a definition of work that contains more pleasure than it would if I had been less fortunate, and which may seem strange to today's urban dwellers and younger people.

Industrial culture has made self-provisioning seem abnormal

Several years ago David Holmgren wrote an apology entitled "From Baby Boomers to the Handicapped Generations":

> *In pioneering the double income family, some of us set the pattern for the next generation's habit of outsourcing the care of children at a young age, making commuting five days a week an early childhood experience. This has left the next generation unable to imagine a life that doesn't involve leaving home each day. These patterns are part of a larger crisis created by the double income, debt-laden households with close to 100% dependence on the monetary economy. Without robust and productive household economies, our children's and grandchildren's generations will become the victims of savage disruptions and downturns in the monetary economy. For failing to maintain and strengthen the threads of self-provision, frugality and self-reliance most of us inherited from our parents, we should be truly sorry. We convinced our children they needed more specialised knowledge poured down their throats rather than using their best years to build the skills and resilience for the challenges our generation was bequeathing to them. For this we must be truly sorry.*[107]

Not only the home but also the school has contributed to passive acceptance of the idea that the most important things happen outside the household. Dimitri Orlov, who moved to this country from Russia as a teenager, sees most of today's children as institutionalized, "humans-Lite," "deprived of the stories, myths and trials that human children have been put through for the past few million years . . . and so are gravely ill-equipped for life outside the artificial life support system. They are an industrial product: almost from birth they are placed in an entirely artificial social context, where they are evaluated, classified, and shoved through a series of institutions to be readied for a lifetime of service in a system whose feedstock is a commodity human product.... Even if their parents and grandparents were intact and able to impart wisdom, the children have not been programmed to process that sort of information."[108]

I can't say whether this is widely true; my own grandchildren were not very institutionalized. They played outdoors in their neighborhoods, saw their parents working at home, and grew up eating meals cooked by one parent or the other together at the family table. I've wondered about the time they spent on screens. But Matthew Crawford writes that the problem of technology is almost the opposite of how the problem is usually posed. For adults as well as children, he says, the problem "is that we've come to live in a world that precisely does not elicit our 'instrumentality,' the embodied kind original to us. We have too few occasions to *do* anything, because of a certain predetermination of things from afar." He tells of the children's "Build A Bear" workshops that purport to let the child build a toy, when actually all the child is able to do is select features and clothes on a computer screen. With today's technology, "some entity has *leaped in* ahead of us and taken care of things already." He points to automobile companies that pay lip service to the customer's desire to do something besides pay money. They say, "Customize your car," and let the buyer select accessories from a small pre-selected group that may, in a programmed way, appeal to different personality types. But as for true engagement with the car, many new models don't even have dipsticks. Tire pressure, oil level—not for the owner to monitor; the car monitors it for us.[109]

Greer calls ours a "prosthetics culture." He writes, "A prosthetic is an artificial device that replaces a human function. They are of course valuable technologies for those that have lost the use of the function in question.... Still, when a society starts convincing people to saw off their own legs so businesses can sell them artificial ones, something has gone decidedly wrong—and that's not too far from the situation we're in today."[110]

Crawford, Orlov, Holmgren, and Greer all advocate for a high level of agency in people's lives, and they fear that those accustomed to not having it will be handicapped in the world of the future. I have the same fear, or I wouldn't be writing on this subject. If the idea of self-provision doesn't arouse excitement in anticipation of the need, perhaps it will as conditions change. Futurist Rob Sheridan said in an interview, "I love classic adventures where people are forced into a task they didn't want to take on and then have to go from their small place in the world out into a much bigger and much more dangerous environment that they never wanted anything to do with."[111]

My goal is to paint a picture of economic contraction that shows the personal expansion it might contain. A list of verbs may point us toward this expanded capacity: beget, breed, bring about, foment, generate, incite, induce, instigate, lead to, precipitate, provoke, spawn, stimulate, stir, create, develop, excite, hatch, make. All are words of action, not of passive acceptance or angry indignation about what is happening to us. They reflect the spirit of a poem I memorized in my English class in the eighth grade.

> *Work!*
> *Thank God for the might of it,*
> *The ardor, the urge, the delight of it—*
> *Work that springs from the heart's desire,*
> *Setting the soul and the brain on fire.*
> *Oh, what is so good as the heat of it,*
> *And what is so glad as the beat of it,*
> *And what is so kind as the stern command*
> *Challenging brain and heart and hand?*
>
> ANGELA MORGAN[112]

In a period of economic and ecological contraction, we will do more work that directly meets our most pressing needs. We will do this not only for the lack of money but for the lack of humans ready to do tasks for us—because those humans will be busy taking care of their own needs. If we are wise, we will of course exchange services, but based on friendship, not money. In such a situation, we will be more bound together than before, due to our need for what others know or have the strength and talent to do. We will share not only out of desire for physical support but also for pleasure and social satisfaction.

If we have developed a sound spiritual practice and formed alliances in which belonging and helping others offer the social and emotional sustenance humans must have from cradle to grave, then we are positioned to take the third step of inner preparation to live well amid radical upheaval. We are ready to acquire the knowledge of how to provide basic life requirements for ourselves and our neighbors.

I will offer information to help us gain confidence on the subjects of food, water, and sanitation. In developed countries most people who can afford it have been paying someone else to grow their food, bring water to their homes, and take away sewage, garbage, and recycling either from their residences or a nearby convenience center. These services meet basic human needs, and yet I'd guess at least two of the three functions are almost complete mysteries to many readers. Food comes from the store, water comes through faucets, and excrement goes out through toilets. End of knowledge.

Most of the rest of the world is not so ignorant. Outside the industrialized countries—and inside many of them—people know how to obtain food other than from the grocery store, find water other than at the home sink, and manage toilet functions other than by peeing in potable water. If the day comes when "someone else" is not there to take away the trash, or if the food grown somewhere else is not accessible, or if the pipes no longer bring water and take away sewage, I want to be ready to do it myself. I must, in order to remain healthy. These are basic human skills necessary for functions that life imposes on us.

Reading an instruction manual is not like reading a novel. Here is how I think you might approach the learning:

1. Read through the material once and picture yourself performing these actions. Some of them you can begin doing immediately, but for other practices, your imagination playing the role first is a good rehearsal for later application.

2. Notice when these skills are mentioned elsewhere, even in your daily life. I find that once I become aware of some approaches to meeting a need, I start hearing others talk about the subject or I come across additional information. Once I begin thinking about water purification or conservation strategies, for example, I'm more likely to notice when other people mention water filters, or when aquifer replenishment pops up in my reading.

3. Go ahead and get copies of the free online materials and the second-hand books suggested in each section. When internet service and easy shipping become less available, we'll need our home libraries to be full of how-to information. Although I hope we have

a little while to get used to doing these things for ourselves before we have to depend on them for our survival, I want us to have handy and helpful support if time presses.

If the curtain begins to come down on the amenities of the industrial era in my lifetime, I hope to be prepared to take care of my most personal and pressing needs. In this third handbook I share my experience and research for self-provision in three categories: food, water, and sanitation. The topics are treated separately, with sub-headings for quick reference.

WHERE WILL OUR FOOD COME FROM?

A consideration of "food miles" may quickly explain why the food supply is likely to become locally sourced. According to government statistics, California's Central Valley produces roughly a quarter of the nation's food and forty percent of its fruits and vegetables. But farmers in that region had to leave nearly 400,000 acres of agricultural land unplanted in 2021 due to a lack of water.[113] In 2023 CNN reported the opposite problem. "Torrents and torrents of rain have drowned thousands of acres of farmland in California's Central Valley this winter and resuscitated a lake that vanished decades ago. As far as the eye can see, water stretches to the horizon — across roads, across crop fields, through homes and buildings."[114] If a large-scale grower can't produce crops dependably year by year due to climate impacts such as drought, flooding, hotter temperatures, insect infestation, absence of pollinators, and fires, that grower can't stay in business, and grocery shelves will be emptied all across the distribution territory. Ordinarily bank loans carry established farmers through hard years, but the financial system will be strained due to mounting costs of climate impacts in many places. I expect the government to provide financial help directly to the largest growers for a while, as a gesture toward containing the extent of hunger in the country, but the difficulties are certain to outlast the money.

Transportation is also a factor. The industrial system moves oil and natural gas around the nation and globe smoothly only when conditions are favorable. In coming years political strife, mass migration, and climate and economic limitations will increasingly make long-distance food sources less accessible.

But with the help of nature and our neighbors, we can grow food for ourselves and our food-producing animals, and we can preserve it to eat in the months between harvests. Some of the skills I mention in the handbook I'll defer to more expert practitioners to explain, but I'll be the primary explainer for food growing, because I consider it the most important knowledge I own. I've been producing most of the vegetables and fruits I eat for a long time. For me the grocery store is where I buy grains and other staples, and I have a plan for growing those in the future, too.

I can say I learned to grow food from my parents, and it's true, although as well as I can remember I never pulled a weed or planted a seed when I was a child. I learned from them, however, as I saw how happily they went out to the garden or field to do those mysterious things. For both of them, it seemed, working with soil and plants was escape from indoor duties. Since they never asked me to help, this work appeared to be adult entertainment. I knew I'd do the same when I grew up, and I looked forward to it.

There are many successful ways to garden, but as with spiritual practice, I'll write only about the methods I know first-hand. I'm growing food now in North Carolina, but because I've gardened in three different climates, my advice will apply to all but the coldest and warmest parts of the United States. In the southernmost growing zones, the planting season is not spring, but fall. In places that still have hard winters, gardeners will need to add infrastructure to protect from cold (see Maine gardener Eliot Coleman's book in the Resources at the end of the chapter). I will write as if the reader had no experience, but I hope advanced food growers will find some new facet here as well. Even after fifty years of growing food, I still read garden lore as if I were a beginner, and I always learn something. Many gardeners seem to share that endless curiosity about plants and how to work with them.

I think the first step in making a garden is to make a mini-compost pile for kitchen scraps in a back corner near the planting space. In this pile I include any plant matter—even a very small amount of paper but not wood—and only imperceptible quantities of meat or dairy. Each time I add fresh material, I cover it with an equal amount of dry matter, usually leaves. This simple, low-labor pile can be left to decompose on its own for a year, or it can be a collection site for the hotter, more complex compost described in the Sanitation section of the handbook.

Preparing permanent beds

When I teach gardening classes, I tell people that soil is the place to begin the instruction—earth as in the name of our planet. For soil is the source of life as surely as is the sun, and both are sacred in cultures that honor true priorities. Our civilization has separated us from earth, but industrial contraction will give us time to reconnect.

The soil we have walked on, though, is not ready to do its magic. The gardener must create the nature preserves we call "beds": pillowy resting places where plant roots can roam and mingle with the resident soil microbes, which the gardener must feed if they are to be healthy and abundant.

Ideally these beds will be located within an easy walk of where you live. I've raised food crops in other people's sunny yards, however, and I've raised part of my vegetables in one yard and part in another, when that was necessary. I'm willing to deal with a lot of hardship in order to eat the way I want to eat, but I'm glad the site of my garden now is only down the hill from where I live. People in cities or living in apartment buildings face special barriers to land access at this time. I predict vacant lots will increasingly become available, as zoning authorities and landlords deal with larger problems. At some point, when nearby parking lots are no longer needed, I expect we'll be removing concrete to put in gardens or building raised beds above the concrete.

In a piece of ground with six or more hours of direct sunlight, I lay out unframed ground-level permanent beds, four feet wide with two-foot paths between. The lines can be curved or straight, but if on an incline, "embrace the hill" to better capture water as it flows downward.

Make the surface of the bed level; you want it to hold onto water, not send it downhill. Raised beds in wood frames look nice but offer no other advantages that I've discovered. If a person cannot bend or kneel, then waist-high boxes at least three feet deep will substitute for the ground. My strategy as I become less nimble is to pair up with younger gardeners. I work now in a community garden, where I contribute by doing tasks that require less stooping.

These beds are never stepped on, and I do not till. The underground world has arranged even hard-packed soil in layers appropriate to plant needs. My role is to add nutrients from above; the soil organisms will take it from there—and with amazing swiftness. They can utilize any plant

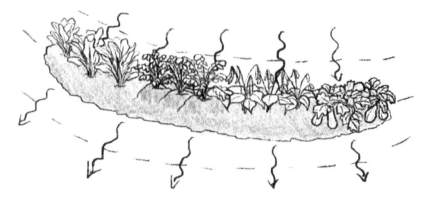

Illustration shows garden bed positioned to catch water coming downward from higher to lower ground.

residue: they eat, digest, and excrete it as porous soil. My practice when creating new beds is to wet the area thoroughly and then lay cardboard on top of the grass and weeds, depriving them of photosynthesis. Several layers of newspaper work as well. The purpose of this first coverage is to wilt on the spot all unwanted plants now growing there, and I'm going to recommend that this preparation be done as soon as the reader thinks "one day I might grow vegetables in that area."

After wetting this covering thoroughly, I leave it in place to soften in dew and rain, weighted down with rocks. I avoid slick printed matter whether on paper or cardboard; the inks are not good for soil-dwellers. Later, when we don't have a surplus of cardboard boxes or paper, I will probably use a tightly packed, four-to-six-inch layer of any dense carbon material that will stay in place, but not wood chips. These I avoid putting on vegetable beds as well as *in* them. Wood in the soil ties up nitrogen (makes it unavailable to plant roots) and if used for mulch, it is hard to set aside all of the chips when planting time comes.

As time allows and materials become available, I recommend adding fallen leaves, unsprayed straw, hay, grass clippings or weeds (prior to flowering) to the cardboard, wetting each application and, if necessary, weighting it down. Each town or city I've lived in has agreed to dump fall-gathered leaves onto my driveway or near it, giving me a year's worth of leaves for beds and compost pile at no cost. Before I discovered that service, I asked for leaves from nearby yards, preferably after they were raked and bagged. I'm sure we'll be gathering leaves from everywhere as city services decline.

I also add soil to the mix—clay subsoil will do in modest amounts. When I don't have another source, I apply topsoil purchased in bags, or I buy it by the cubic yard and have it hauled to my property. At some point I add manure: no uncomposted animal feces, including human, and never cat poop or litter, because cat feces may contain toxoplasmosis eggs. At the present time we can buy cow manure in bags, and as long as we have such soil amendments available, we should use them when we can't get barnyard droppings. I've heard warnings that some bagged manure contains harmful chemicals that remain in the soil for a long time. I didn't have that experience in the years when, as a city gardener, I couldn't find other manures, but perhaps that's yet another way our world is becoming more toxic.

Once I've created a layer of soil an inch thick, and enough time has lapsed for the cardboard underneath to break down considerably, I can plant many types of vegetables in that bed. Ideally I'd wait a year. The waiting period gives soil life a chance to congregate in that area; the covering materials invite them to a carbon feast.

Because I think everyone should begin now, while we still have sources of commercially prepared organic fertilizer ingredients, I will share a formula based on a recipe by Steve Solomon:[115] 4 parts seed meal, 1 part ground limestone, 1 part finely ground rock phosphate or bone meal, ¼ part gypsum, and half that much kelp meal. I keep a 5-gallon bucket of this mix, stirred so thoroughly I can't identify any single ingredient, ready to use at all times. When we can no longer buy these nutrients from a store, I plan to proceed with Joseph Jenkins's fertilizer plan, which includes the composting of humanure, explained in the Sanitation section of this handbook. But don't worry. By that time we'll be doing many things we can't yet imagine ourselves able to do.

I sprinkle the dry mixture somewhat sparingly on the entire bed before planting a crop, enough to show a fine white coloring, which I rake in lightly. This combination suits the soils in areas with rainfall abundant enough to grow forests. The soil in arid parts of the country would not need to be limed, and if your area tends to be short on magnesium, I'd add ¼ part dolomitic limestone.

Selecting important vegetables

I recommend beginning with five highly reliable, nutrient-dense vegetables with good storage qualities. In most of the United States the following should grow well in a warming climate: Irish potatoes, Swiss chard, southern cowpeas, sweet potatoes, and alliums (onions and garlic).

- Irish potatoes. Boiling-type potatoes (as contrasted with the brown-skin baking potato) with good storage qualities and conditions can provide protein for several months after harvest without refrigeration.
- Swiss chard, a cold-tolerant biennial, will provide fresh leafy greens continuously all year, except in the hottest or coldest weather, when it will seem to falter. You can store this vegetable in the ground: leave it in the bed and it will grow again until it bolts (sends up a seed stalk) more than a year after planting.
- Cowpeas grow easily in all the warmer months, and they furnish the soil with nitrogen when they are cut down. For taste I recommend Pinkeye Purple Hull or other crowder types. They can be preserved by drying, the easiest method of food preservation.
- Sweet potatoes may be the most rewarding crop for time invested. They mature in just over three months in summer, and after maturity can be stored at room temperature for eight or nine months.
- Alliums: Onions and garlic. Although day length type and planting date have to be considered when choosing a variety of bulbing onion, these and garlic grow with little attention from the gardener other than weeding from planting time in November until maturity the next summer. Both keep for months after harvest.

In the far north and in the mountains, cowpeas can be replaced by the green pea that my Southern-bred mother called the English pea and the rest of the world calls simply "pea." The bush form is a shell pea, but there is also the delicious climbing pea that can be eaten shell and all, the original and best variety being Sugar Snap. Sweet potatoes can be replaced by one of the root vegetables that thrives in cool weather: carrot, beet, turnip, and rutabaga. All of these roots can be kept fresh and eaten over several months when stored at temperatures just above freezing.

Two other high-nutrient vegetables I would recommend if you have space are green beans (they used to be called string beans because they used to have strings), and butternut squash. Green beans, which come in both bush and pole varieties, require almost daily picking, but with adequate moisture a majority of the plants will bear throughout the growing season. Butternut squash has few requirements other than full sun and room to roam. A vine can be fifteen feet long and is best grown on the ground so that it can root along the stem: these additional roots gather moisture and nutrients from the soil, and I've read the method also gives the plant a chance to survive if a vine borer attacks. The borer can be removed from that bad section without losing the entire plant. I plant *Cucurbita moschata* because borers don't seem to bother it. I bake the squash whole and then split it lengthwise and clean out the seed cavity while it's warm. A Waltham—a large, open-pollinated variety—can weigh five or six pounds; one provides abundant servings for several people. One vine can produce a dozen squashes in good soil and sun.

I didn't include on the list the veggies found most frequently in home gardens: tomatoes, peppers, and lettuce. People should grow them if they have time and room; all three are delightful additions to diet. But I'm growing food as sustenance. I aim at nutrient density per square foot and a long period of eating for my labor. For health we need bone-and-muscle food, and while I myself don't rely on plants for all of my protein, I want to get all the nourishment possible from the vegetable garden.

SWISS CHARD

When the bed is ready for planting, seeds of Swiss chard might be the first to go into the ground. The hardiest variety—with plants, hardy means cold-tolerant, not rugged—is the original dark green Fordhook Giant, but the newer colorfully-stemmed varieties also grow well and are widely adapted. Follow package directions for spacing and depth, but in general, planting depth depends on seed size: the larger the deeper, and depth is double the seed width. Swiss chard will live through hot summers and cold winters, but for constant harvest quality, give it cover when temperatures are much below freezing. At present we use spun-bonded row covers designed to give frost protection. When these aren't available, we may mulch heavily and wait for the new growth of spring.

Readers who haven't lived in the US South may not be familiar with cooked greens (Swiss chard, like spinach, is high in oxalic acid and should be cooked to remove it). The simplest way to cook them is in a covered pan with a little water for a few minutes. Cooked greens and a baked potato with butter make a fine and easy supper.

IRISH POTATOES

Potatoes are planted next, and they have a unique growing pattern. Irish potatoes are not grown from seed but from sprouted tubers. As long as they are available we should buy certified disease-free seed potatoes for our Irish potato crops. *Solanum tuberosum* is prone to disease in second or third generations, and while someday we may have to grow our own "seed," by that time I hope we will know more about preventing disease.

Several weeks before planting, I buy certified seed potatoes and set them in a single layer in light but not direct sunlight. Resting in their boxes, these potatoes will begin to sprout, and their little green buds are the start of a new vine.

A day or two before planting I cut the large ones into approximately two-ounce sections with two sprouted eyes in each section. A small potato can be planted whole. I plant each potato section four inches deep, sprouts up, twelve inches apart in rows 36 inches apart. Four-foot beds allow for two rows, a yard apart. The sprouts will soon begin to grow into vines, which are very frost sensitive. Last year we lost most of our crop when the spring temperature surprised us and fell to freezing long after our traditional last frost date. We won't take that risk again; with this painful reminder that predictions aren't always right, we will cover the beds if we expect it to be colder than 40°F.

When the potato vines are eight inches high, the lower four inches need to be "hilled up," or buried in soil or other dense but not impervious material, such as shredded leaves or hay or a combination. I begin by pulling soil from between the rows onto the vines, using a hoe. Buried vines will bear tiny new potatoes all along their below-ground stems; all the tubers form above the original seed section. Throughout their growing period, this growing area must be protected from light to prevent greening of the tubers, and it must be enlarged upward by some means so that many potatoes will have room to form. By harvest time each vine will be surrounded by a mound. A major advantage of growing our own potatoes is to avoid the greened ones sold by grocery stores. Greening is caused by exposure to light, and greened potatoes can cause solanine poisoning.

Potatoes need even moisture until tubers begin to size up. At that point I withhold extra watering so that the potatoes will be dense and protein rich. I always hope it won't rain a lot at the end; they keep better if harvested when soil and air are drier. When most of the vines in the bed have begun to look tired—yellowed and not growing—it's probably time to harvest. In order not to damage the potatoes, we slip the shovel very carefully under the center of the vine from the outside edge. At that point we work by hand, shaking the vine to loosen the soil and reaching with our hands or hand tool to find all the potatoes the vine has produced. Handle carefully; the skins are delicate for a day or so, and undamaged potatoes store longer.

One more detail: fertilizer for Irish potatoes should have no lime and be low in potassium. Omit the lime from the mixture and be sure not to add wood ash to this bed. In this short introduction to food growing I'm not advising about wood ash, coffee grounds, or any of the popular amendments of folklore; before you use them, investigate!

SOUTHERN COWPEAS

Southern cowpeas, also called crowder peas or field peas, are planted after the average last frost date. Most people know about black-eyed peas; to me they are fairly tasteless, and chefs usually add onions or peppers to make them palatable. The Pinkeye Purple Hull and similar crowder varieties need only salt, although southern cooks have traditionally added salt pork to the pot. We eat cowpeas in bowls in order to enjoy the thickened broth that forms as they cook. Cowpeas should be cooked until they're very soft, and to be sure they'll be soupy, fill the covered pan with at least an inch of water above the peas.

Bigger seed, plant deeper. I plant these in two rows nearer the middle of the bed because they sprawl. This year we plan to grow them on a short fence, to make picking easier and to keep them off the paths. We eat most of the crop fresh, but also raise enough to freeze some for winter eating, and we also can several pints each year to have on hand in case the electricity goes out. Although the easiest way to store crowder peas is to dry them, in our humid climate a dehydrator or a long drying period in open jars is required to prevent mold formation.

SWEET POTATOES

Sweet potatoes, like the Irish potatoes described above, are planted from sprouted tubers, not from seed—but in this case only the sprouts are planted. Since *Ipomoea batatas* is not as vulnerable to disease as *Solanum tuberosum*, I use sprouts from one year's crop to plant the next year. To plant the first time, you will probably buy sprouted plants from a garden center or feed store. Or you can try to sprout the tubers you bought for eating. We sprout ours in an open box in a warm place, no soil, no water. They sprout almost automatically when they're about a year old, so plan in advance.

Sweet potatoes need fairly loose soil, not especially rich. Sandy soils are ideal. The plants are highly drought tolerant, and the primary maintenance chore is restraining the vigorous vines. I put a fence around the bed so that people can walk on the paths. The vines don't climb, they sprawl widely. The leaves are edible, too, although they aren't my preferred greens. Eating the growing vines could be a way to keep them in check, but leave enough vine to feed the roots.

Like Irish potatoes, sweet potatoes are dug all at once, but they need a longer growing period—about a hundred days. Dig before first frost regardless of size and place in shallow boxes to "cure," handling as little as possible. They need air, preferably as warm as 85°F., for about ten days in order for the starches to turn to sugar. They will then keep at room temperature until time to plant again the next spring.

ONIONS AND GARLIC

Alliums are a special case. The must-do for bulbing onions is to plant a variety suited to the garden's latitude. Here at 35° latitude I plant intermediate-day-length varieties. My friend in Atlanta plants short-day; in Minnesota I would plant long-day types. The other trick is to get them in the ground at the right time. I usually plant seeds in fall for overwintering in the ground; onions can survive low temperatures with little protection once they are established. In order for them to bulb instead of bolt in the spring, Steve Solomon advises their stems should be no thicker than a pencil when winter sets in to halt the green stage of their growth. At this time in the Southeast US that means I start the seeds by the end of August and put them in the ground the first of November. Climate change will alter that schedule, I'm sure.

I choose storage-type varieties, and usually start the seeds in flats (wide shallow containers that allow for many plants to emerge from seed). If I'm also planting some in spring, I start those in January and keep the flats on a south-facing porch until they're ready to go into the bed. From that location I can cover them well or bring them inside on very cold nights. Plant as shallowly as possible for larger onions. They need the richest soil of all these five vegetables, they need even moisture until they reach the bulbing stage, and at no stage do they like soggy feet.

Home gardeners usually plant garlic from cloves bought from a quality dealer. I separate the garlic head into its sections, and each section becomes the "seed" for a new head of garlic. I set the cloves in the ground in November, pointed end up, and harvest the following June when the tops begin to die—but before the underground cloves begin to separate on their own. In my location I can plant either softneck (braidable) or hardneck garlic (with a rigid center stalk), but I prefer hardneck for flavor and keeping quality. Our high humidity means the heads begin to shrivel in dry storage before the next planting year, which means I plan to learn to grow garlic from the seeds known as bulbils that form at the top of a hardneck stalk. I've read that it may take three years for a small bulbil to grow into a proper head of garlic, so I'll experiment with this method while I can still purchase seed garlic from a dealer. Grocery store garlic might be disease free, but I can't know whether it is or not. As with potatoes, I will rely on certified seed stock as long as it's available.

In our community garden we grow many more crops than I listed above, but here I emphasize survival food—producing the most nutritious food with the least effort. I hope gardeners will branch out in time, always doing some research beforehand. Before I started my first large garden I read every book in my local library on the topic; not a minute of that education was wasted time. Used-book classics now cost just a few dollars. A short list of good ones is at the end of the Food section.

I'm gradually switching from hybrid to open-pollinated seed, since I think it will become harder to buy seed in the future and I'll need to provide my own. A hybrid plant is formed when the male part of one plant's flower pollinates the female part of a different variety of flower. The result may produce a stronger plant, but seed from it will not reproduce predictably. This level of plant breeding might be done by anyone with a lot of time and patience, but it will be quicker to locate a reliable open-pollinated variety. Open-pollination seed will breed true if it's the only variety of that vegetable within pollinator range. By "breed true," I mean I can expect the same qualities from the child as in the parent.

Seed-saving for excellent results is a specialized study—knowledge

I aim to acquire in greater depth while there is time. I will study the requirements for the most vital crops, which for me will be the seven I've mentioned plus beets, carrots, more cooking greens, several beans or peas, and brassicas such as kale and some variety of the large heading cabbages that have been the standby of gardens for a long time. Perhaps if I live long enough I'll get into plant breeding, to improve on the few good open-pollinated varieties still purchasable, or to convert a hybrid variety to open-pollinated by careful plant selection over a few years.

Caring for garden vegetable plants

Water. Growing vegetables need soil, sun, water, and protection from predators. In the Water section of this handbook I describe several landscaping strategies that help the soil collect and hold the moisture that arrives in the form of precipitation. In my own gardening I focus on avoiding moisture loss so that I have less watering to do. We use several of these strategies for our community garden, and even during drought we don't often irrigate mature plants. We mulch everything—no bare soil!—sometimes with just weighted-down cardboard or newspaper.

At present our garden's water source is two 250-gallon rainwater catchment tanks located some distance up the hill, and we move water down to the garden with hoses. Since our garden is large, we don't move the hoses from bed to bed very often, but instead keep plastic milk jugs filled so that we can hand carry water to far-flung beds that hold seeds or transplants or young seedlings.

Other water-wise techniques:

- Wider plant spacing allows roots to roam farther in search of below-ground moisture.
- Watering deeply but less often encourages roots to go downward rather than laterally where there is more evaporation.
- A rough time for vegetables regarding water is a period of dryness following a long period of rain. Abundant moisture tends to encourage roots to stay near the surface. Weekly deep watering for a while may be necessary in order to redirect root growth downward.
- Some plants require more water than others. I focus on drought-tolerant vegetables and ornamentals. In the suggested group, only Irish potatoes are finicky about moisture, and I only give them supplemental watering during the tuber-growth period.

VEGETABLE	GROWING SEASON ZONE 7	TYPE SEED	GROWTH STYLE	FERTILIZATION NEEDS	MOISTURE NEEDS	PRESERVATION METHOD
Irish potatoes	March to June	tubers	underground in mounds	average, no lime	regular, drier near harvest	dry cool storage
Swiss chard	March to March	seeds	above ground	average	drought tolerant	fresh
Cowpeas	May to October	seeds	above ground, vining to 5 feet	average	drought tolerant	dried
Sweet potatoes	May to September	sprouts of tubers	underground	average	drought tolerant	dry storage, room temperature
Bulbing onions	November to June	seeds	underground	high	regular, drier near harvest	dry cool storage
Garlic	November to June	cloves	underground	average to high	regular, drier near harvest	dry cool storage
Green beans	April to October	seeds	above ground, with or without support	average	regular	Fresh, canned, frozen, dried
Butternut squash	May to October	seeds	above ground, vining to 15 feet	average to high	regular	dry storage, room temperature

Companion plants. Vegetables grow best among herbs, flowers, and wild plants, preferably natives in order to attract resident pollinators and the insects whose larvae feed birds, which eat predators. I've never observed the benefit of planting a particular flower as companion to a particular vegetable, but it's easy to see that plants flourish in mixed groups rather than as individuals as long as each has its needs met for sun and moisture.

Security. The vegetables I'm suggesting have another survivalist quality: none are conspicuous enough to attract undue attention—except maybe the wide-ranging butternuts with their large yellow blossoms. If hunger becomes more widespread in a culture where few people grow food, I wouldn't put temptation in the path, i.e., grow cantaloupes or tomatoes on the curbside. And just as I wouldn't brag about how much money I kept under the mattress, I wouldn't advertise my prowess at growing food. We do want to share the surplus when we have it, but I would set up my stand somewhere away from my residence, or donate to a food pantry.

Fencing. Because well-tended vegetable plants are highly desirable to animals other than humans, I always put a fence around them. If you don't have deer, a perimeter of two-foot high, one-inch mesh chicken wire is a good barrier for animals that don't climb. You don't need a gate at that height; just step over. When I don't have deer, however, my preference is to use five-or-six-foot welded wire fencing that would support vining crops like tomatoes and pole beans. Deer fencing is not only too flimsy for heavy vines, but it also puts climbing vegetables up at a handy height for deer to eat. To protect crops from squirrels, raccoons, and birds requires protection above as well as around. We use bird netting (be certain it's the kind birds can't get caught in) supported by posts of the required height. When I've had voles, I've had to protect root crops by surrounding them with cages made with one-inch-mesh hardware cloth. With groundhogs—vegetarians that eat eight times a day and can both dig and climb—the only protection is a live-animal trap and hauling the animal ten miles away. Note: these products are industrial amenities that may be hard to find in the future. Stock up!

Insects. Here in the US Southeast we have many insects that like to eat our vegetables. On the crops I'm suggesting here, the first insects to appear might be potato bugs. The Colorado potato beetle is a pretty bug about a half inch long, with orange head and shoulders and a rounded back with striped creamy white and black stripes running front to back. After our potato vines are a foot or so tall and the weather is quite warm, we start checking the plants every day. When we find one of the beetles, we pick it off into a small jar of detergent water. We also do this with the Japanese beetles that come for six weeks or so in the summer and feed on many kinds of plants. The other crop we watch closely is squash, and the villain we look for here is the squash bug: dark gray to dark brown, flat-backed, just over a half-inch long, and shield-shaped, like the stink bug but with a different pattern on its back. They are attracted to members of the squash families, but once there are a great number, they will eat anything. Because they are so destructive, if we see one in the garden, we begin checking the undersides of the large butternut squash leaves for clusters of the bright gold-to-russet-colored eggs. We crush the eggs and drop bugs into detergent water, as with potato beetles. But as I said earlier, we grow butternuts because they are less likely than other squashes to attract these pests.

Alliums and Swiss chard don't seem to attract many damaging insects, although I've read about allium leaf miners and onion maggots, and have seen a long list of possible pests of chard. Where I live, fire ants are the most unpleasant garden-area pests. Because they eat small seeds (as well as take bites out of gardeners), we now start most seedlings— even beets and corn— in seed trays and then transplant. To discourage the ant hill, we scoop out the center with a shovel (taking that dirt away from the garden) and fill the hole with diatemaceous earth. Experience tells me to expect a new insect or animal to appear tomorrow, however, or next year. I try to run my eyes over every bed every day, looking for signs of health, sickness, or invasion.

Degrees of difficulty. To be truthful, it does seem harder every year to grow the food we eat. As the whole of nature struggles, we can't expect the domesticated crops of our gardens to be spared the difficulties. More heat, more insects of the kind we don't want but perhaps fewer of the insect allies, uneven rainfall if we are blessed to have it at all—these are the circumstances in which many readers will be beginning their food-producing careers. From childhood I've known how helpless a farmer can feel as crops wither and fail. I remember seeing my father in the middle of a field with his arms in the air, fists clenched, as he saw rain falling on the nearby road but not a drop onto his crop.

Yet farming families want to stay to plant another year. They love the land and they love the way of life it provides. For me and my garden partners there are reasons to keep tending soil and planting seeds besides the growing of what we ourselves eat. As we protect and nourish the soil, we are leaving a legacy to creatures who come after us in this place, and we are storing carbon in the ground rather than emitting it. Those of us with access to land can endeavor to leave it in better condition than we found it, regardless of whether we grow food on it. Industrial agriculture has done the opposite. We can replace exploitation with caring attention and enjoy some good meals as we do.

Additional resources:

Get acquainted with your state's extension service. The North Carolina Cooperative Extension Service of NC State University and NC A&T University has developed a planting calendar for farmers and gardeners in this area. The website offers helpful discussions of suitable varieties of almost any plant a person might want to grow, including trees and flowers. Services of this kind exist in every state; they are an obligation of the Smith–Lever Act of 1914, when Congress recognized the need to "disseminate the knowledge gained at the land-grant colleges to farmers and homemakers."[116] Each county has extension service agents as well, available to answer individual queries. The universities primarily serve "big agriculture," but extension agents and departments have gradually become open to organic methods and home gardening. Again, use them while we have them.

> Carol Deppe, *Breed Your Own Vegetables: The Gardener's and Farmer's Guide to Plant Breeding and Seed Saving* (White River Junction, VT: Chelsea Green, 1993).
>
> Deppe, *The Resilient Gardener: Food Production and Self-Reliance in Uncertain Times* (White River Junction, VT: Chelsea Green, 2010).
>
> Colorado State Extension Service, https://extension.colostate.edu/topic-areas/yard-garden/vegetable-gardening-in-the-mountains-7-248/.
>
> Eliot Coleman, *Four-Season Harvest* (White River Junction, VT: Chelsea Green, 1992).
>
> Masanobu Fukuoka, *One Straw Revolution: The Natural Way of Farming* (Emmaus PA: Rodale Press, 1978).
>
> Nancy Bubel with Jean Nick, *The New Seed-Starter's Handbook* (Emmaus PA: Rodale Press, 2018).
>
> Seed Savers Exchange, https://www.seedsavers.org. The website says, "SSE stewards America's culturally diverse and endangered garden and food crop legacy for present and future generations. We educate and connect people through collecting, regenerating, and sharing heirloom seeds, plants, and stories."
>
> Steve Solomon, *Gardening When It Counts: Growing Food in Hard Times* (Gabriola Island: New Society Publishers, 2005).
>
> Solomon, *The Intelligent Gardener: Growing Nutrient-Dense Food* (Gabriola Island: New Society Publishers, 2013).

Solomon, The Soil and Health Library soilandhealth.org. The website says it "provides free downloadable e-books about radical agriculture, natural hygiene/nature cure and self-sufficiency. There are secondary collections involving social criticism and transformational psychology. Topic areas connect agricultural methods to the health and lifespan of animals and humans. A study of these materials reveals how to prevent and heal disease and increase longevity, suggests how to live a more fulfilling life and reveals social forces working against that possibility. There is no fee for downloading anything in the library."

Southern Exposure Seed Exchange, https://www.southernexposure.com. Their mission statement is "We encourage cooperative self-reliance in agriculture. We promote and participate in seed saving and exchange, ecological agriculture, reducing energy use, providing locally adapted varieties, and regional food production."

Suzanne Ashworth, *Seed to Seed: Seed Saving and Growing Techniques for Vegetable Gardeners* (Decorah, IA: Seed Savers Exchange, 2002).

Toby Hemenway, *Gaia's Garden: A Guide to Home-Scale Permaculture* (White River Junction, VT: Chelsea Green, 2000).

HOW WILL WE MEET OUR NEED FOR CLEAN WATER?

My heart is heavy when I consider the problem of meeting water needs in coming decades. In areas that will be increasingly desert-like due to climate change, the problem will be scarcity, but even in places with high rainfall, towns and cities may not be able to provide the infrastructure maintenance required for safe community water systems. People have managed to live in arid regions throughout history, but with lifestyles radically different from the way Americans now live in the drying US West and Southwest. Most of the world's people, past and present, have lived without the pipes and sewage systems on which a majority of readers may now depend, but homes that depend on them become uninhabitable when these amenities are unreliable. Learning to obtain water to meet human water needs for drinking and sanitation has to be high on the list of preparedness skills. And humans won't survive long anywhere if the surrounding natural world doesn't get its share of moisture. In short, with or without community water systems, most of us need to learn where our water comes from now, where it will come from in a period of institutional collapse, and how to transport, distribute, and conserve it peacefully and with fairness among all users.

A 2022 article in the *New York Times* climate newsletter began, "Cities around the world are being forced to live with less water, as global warming melts glaciers, diminishes snowpacks and exacerbates decades of water mismanagement. Not just less water for now. Maybe less water forever."[117] Less water forever. According to the 2018 edition of the United Nations World Water Development Report, more than half of humanity will suffer from the lack of fresh water by 2050. An argument could be made that water scarcity will be the biggest problem the world faces in the future.

At the present time, water quality rather than water scarcity is the major concern for many people in the United States. Water is piped into my home according to code for homes built inside the limits of our very small town, which buys it from a larger town nearby. We're not perfectly satisfied with the quality, but it runs clear, and the water-sewer system is diligently maintained. We know personally our maintenance director and the maintenance crew. I feel fortunate.

Community water systems now face significant problems

City water systems have been around for a long time. The Minoan civilization in Crete had flushing toilets and domestic water as early as 1700 B.C. Ancient Rome, with a population close to 1 million people at its height, brought in water so skillfully from the nearby countryside through those famous Roman aqueducts that residents of Rome had something like 100 gallons per person per day at their disposal, an amount comparable to what affluent modern cities supply.[118]

At this point I have to admit my own knowledge about water systems is a recent interest, based on my sense that our time of easy abundance is under threat. A realistic strategy for obtaining the water we need for living will capture and protect water at each stage of Earth's hydrologic cycle. Our lives may depend on this knowledge.[119]

In most climates, and increasingly everywhere, precipitation will mainly fall in the form of rain. We can capture rainwater on the land where it falls, protect it from evaporation, and direct the excess into the ground, where it will eventually refill aquifers.

Groundwater may become our direct source of water

Wells. People whose homes are not connected to community watering systems usually depend upon groundwater, most often obtained by means of wells. Wells still supply water to 99% of the US rural population.[120] When I was a child, a man named Johnny Moreland was the local well digger. He worked by hand, using a platform that was lowered and raised by a rope and pulley set in a strong frame that would, once the well was dug, hold the bucket that would be used to bring up water for drinking. The soil he dug as he descended was periodically drawn up on the platform by his helper at the surface.

In *Peak Oil Survival*, Aric McBay gives instructions for hand digging that type of well.[121] McBay begins by warning that the first consideration is "will there be water?". He advises digging when the groundwater level is likely to be low—at the end of the driest season in your area—and in locations where the water table is likely to be high. To help answer the latter question, the community we live in now hired a dowser, who found three likely sites within the area we had chosen. We've flagged the sites and started "a permanent water source" fund and a committee to consider all possibilities, including to bring water uphill from the river that borders one side of the community land, or the creek that borders the other.

We realize that drilling a well is not a guarantee of good drinking water, and we will have the water tested if we drill while testing is easy to obtain. Much of our groundwater is now polluted by landfills, septic tanks, leaky underground gas tanks, and from overuse of fertilizers and pesticides. Earlier I mentioned the well at my grandparents' East Texas farm in my childhood; I said it was the sweetest water in the world, and that may have been true. After the grandparents died, my own parents moved out to the old homeplace, and when I visited them I used to take empty gallon jugs with me so I could carry that well's water back to Kansas City to enjoy for a week or two. The sad story, though, is that after East Texas became a thriving oilfield, the groundwater in the area became so saturated with salt that the region's water became almost undrinkable—drinking it created thirst. Their well might as well have gone dry.

In the US West, both groundwater and surface water are guarded by water rights based on treaties that direct the flow toward large users. In Colorado, for example, if you have a well (not municipal water) that was drilled after May 2, 1972, and your property is less than 35 acres, you may not have any outdoor water rights. You may not legally use water from your well for your garden or store rainwater in barrels. Well drilling is closely regulated, with rules varying from state to state.

Everywhere, however, wise water practices begin with abundant groundwater, and the fact that rainwater harvesting interferes with the natural water cycle should be kept in mind. The overall objective of water management is to nourish groundwater.

Groundwater recharge. All over the world at this time humans are learning methods for groundwater recharge. It is a rich field of study, too broad for this introduction to water provisioning, but a list of online resources and the areas they address can be a stimulant to our impoverished imaginations. Water at our fingertips has allowed us not to know how most of the world obtains water, and it has been encouraging to me to discover how much creativity is being invested to save whatever available fresh water falls into each geographic location, even as climate change increases the challenges.

- The Wikiversity site covering aquifer storage and recovery (ASR—a specific type of groundwater recharge practiced with the purpose of both augmenting ground water resources and recovering the water in the future for various uses) explains the following practices: infiltration ponds; contour trenches and ridges; bunds (an embankment used to control the flow of water); dams of permeable rock; sand dams; gully plugs or check dams; leaky dams; gabions (a kind of check dam commonly constructed across small streams to conserve stream flows with practically no submergence beyond stream course); spreading basins; tube recharge; infiltration; and wells, boreholes, and shafts. (https://en.wikiversity.org/wiki/Stormwater_harvesting_and_management/Groundwater_recharge.)

- Vikaspedia, available in English but primarily serving the population of India, describes most of these measures but also offers strategies for urban areas that direct surplus water from rooftops into aquifers rather than into surface containers. These include recharge pits and trenches, tube wells, and trenches with recharge wells. (https://vikaspedia.in/energy/environment/rainwater-harvesting-1/rain-water-harvesting-techniques-to-augment-ground-water.)

- Natural Water Retention Measures is a project of the European Union to help achieve and maintain healthy water ecosystems. In agricultural areas, techniques include buffer strips and hedges, crop rotation, strip cropping along contours, intercropping, no till agriculture, traditional terracing, reduced stock density, and mulching. In urban settings the practices advocated but not mentioned already include green roofs, permeable surfaces, channels and rills, filter strips, soakaways, infiltration trenches, and rain gardens. There are also wise use suggestions for forests, as well as for ponds and streams. (http://nwrm.eu/measures-catalogue.)

- Roads for Water is an intriguing initiative that emphasizes the harvesting of water that falls onto roadways. Its 2025 goal is that 50% of all roads will be instruments of beneficial water management and resilience in at least 50% of the countries in Africa and in 25% of countries in Asia. (https://roadsforwater.org/guideline/.)

As with many of the technologies mentioned in this water section of the handbook, most models for action have arisen first in less developed countries. Information about groundwater recharge is shared on the internet at present, and since aquifer levels where most of us live have been lowered by industrial processes, it would be important to lay claim to this knowledge—and make print copies of detailed instructions—now. Techniques for storing water in the land such as those I describe later in the water discussion also serve the goal of groundwater recharge.

Water purification will be an important skill to acquire

Whether household water comes from a well or a tap—from groundwater or from a community system that accesses surface water—it may not be safe for all uses. Even if we capture rainwater as it falls, we will need to purify it for drinking.

WATER PURIFICATION: CARBON FILTERS

The two most common types of filtration for residential use are reverse osmosis and activated carbon filters. At our house currently we filter the water coming through the faucet using a Berkey filter system. Berkey claims their carbon filters remove 99.9% of contaminants, including pathogenic bacteria and viruses. Minerals such as calcium, sodium, potassium, and magnesium pass through the filter. Other filters may meet NSF/ANSI 61 standards and yet be less expensive.[122]

One do-it-yourself arrangement employs two BPA-free, food-grade 5-gallon buckets in the same pattern as the Berkey (see illustration below). This pattern calls for two stacked containers with filters in the top container. The DIY design attaches two Berkey-style filters to the bottom of the upper bucket by drilling holes to fit, with matching holes in the lid of the lower bucket. Water from any source is put into the upper bucket, where it seeps through the filters and passes down their inner chambers into the lower bucket. The design calls for a spigot to be installed near the base of the lower bucket, as in the Berkey system, and uses a gamma seal lid on the top bucket instead of the regular lid, for ease of opening to refill. The gamma seal's gasket is affixed to the outer rim of the lid to make it air-and-water tight, and the lid bears a raised criss-cross design on the surface to give a good handhold so there's no need to pry the lid open.

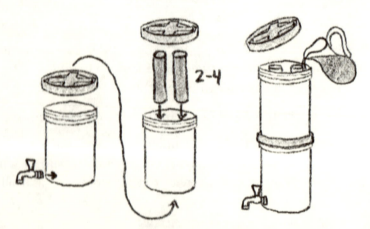

Water is poured into top bucket, filtered through the charcoal cylinders, and gradually collected in the lower bucket where it is released through the spigot.

These small-scale units can improve the quality of water flowing from a community water system, but they can also purify even dirty water to make it safe to drink. They could be used, for example, to filter rainwater harvested from the roof. Homes generally have a gutter-and-downspout installation to carry rainwater that falls on the roof away from the foundation. A "barrel" equipped with a spigot, set beneath a shortened downspout, provides a simple catchment that can be expanded by setting a series of barrels with successively lower outflow valves. A rain barrel is fairly simple to set up; I've done it, and I'm not much of an engineer (instructions below in the Water Storage section). This unfiltered water is ready for many applications, and it can also be filtered for drinking. Charcoal filters are easy to find at present, and they are long-lasting if the water being filtered is relatively clean. Water containing debris can be strained through a cloth prior to passing through the filters.

EFFECTIVENESS IN REMOVAL[1]

TYPE	PROTOZOA	BACTERIA	VIRUSES	CHEMICALS	PORE SIZE
Microfiltration	Very high	Moderate	Not effective	Not effective	0.1 micron
Ultrafiltration	Very high	Very high	Moderate	Low	0.1 micron
Nanofiltration	Very high	Very high	Very high	Moderate	0.001 micron
Reverse Osmosis	Very high	Very high	Very high	Very high[2]	0.0001 micron

[1]The treatment technologies described can be used in conjunction with each other for greater pathogen reduction. The addition of coagulants, carbon, alum, and iron salts to filtration systems may aid in chemical removal from water.

²Reverse osmosis systems will remove common chemical contaminants (metal ions, aqueous salts), including sodium, chloride, copper, chromium, and lead; may reduce arsenic, fluoride, radium, sulfate, calcium, magnesium, potassium, nitrate, and phosphorous.[123]

WATER PURIFICATION: BIOSAND FILTRATION

In a chaotic economic setting, however, the materials for filtering water through biosand may be more available than charcoal filters. The Sustainable Sanitation and Water Management Toolbox describes the method in these words: "A biosand filter consists of a concrete or plastic container filled with specially selected and prepared sand and gravel. As water flows through the filter, physical straining removes pathogens, iron, turbidity and manganese from drinking water. A shallow layer of water sits atop the sand and a biofilm (Schmutzdecke) develops. The biofilm contributes to the removal of pathogens due to predation and competition for food of non-harmful microorganisms contained in the biofilm and the harmful organisms in the water."[124] It takes 20 to 30 days for the Schmutzdecke to form, and because the bacteria require moisture to survive, water should be added daily during this period.

CAWST, a Canadian charity and licensed engineering firm that provides training in water and sanitation in developing countries, has published a complete guide to building biosand filters, including preparation of the sand and gravel. The CAWST training manual for "Design, Construction, Installation, Operation, and Maintenance" of the biosand filter recommends crushed rock as the best type of filtration sand, "since it has less chance of being contaminated with pathogens or organic material. This sand also has less uniform sizing of the grains. A mixture of grain sizes is required for the proper functioning of the filter. Gravel pits or quarries are the best place to obtain crushed rock, and are common in most parts of the world. . . . Crushed rock may be difficult to locate, more expensive, and require transportation to your production site. However, it is critical in providing the best water quality and is worth the extra time, effort and cost. If crushed rock is absolutely not available, the next choice is sand from high on the banks of a river (that has not been in the water), followed by sand found in the riverbed itself. The last choice is beach sand."[125]

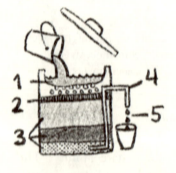

Sand filter pattern based on CAWST guide
1 Dirty water to be filtered
2 Biological layer, kills most pathogens
3 Layers of sand and gravel (lowest)
4 Outlet for purified water
5 Purified water, safe to drink

    I encourage everyone to read and print the entire CAWST manual, which at the time of this writing is the September 2009 Edition. The portion of the manual pertaining to obtaining and preparing the sand is included in Appendix III. I'm not including instructions for building the concrete mold or filter box, since you might decide to utilize plastic buckets or other containers, such as the IBC tote pictured below, but I am including preparation of the diffuser, because the requirements for it would need to be applied to a diffuser of any other shape.

    I've seen a larger and more elegant biosand rainwater filtration system in the off-grid home of the designer-builder located not far from where we live. Built on-site, its owner calls it "a resilient way to establish water security in uncertain times." He told me, "We use a series of three rainwater harvesting tanks made from IBC totes (see illustration) as the rainwater collection tank, with biological slow sand filter tank design and a site-built underground concrete cistern that utilizes the foundation walls of our storage shed (with a concrete floor and concrete tank floor) to hold 10,000 gallons of clean rainwater." Plans are available from Heirloom Builders.[126]

IBC totes similar to the one in the illustration are now widely available at a reasonable cost.

Water from the third 300-gallon tank that has been filtered through biosand is piped into their house. They don't drink water directly from the cistern; they store water there in case of prolonged drought.

At this time he gets the sand and gravel from a supplier in Eau Claire, Wisconsin.[127] His system uses the following quantities, for a total cost at this writing of $1,052.55:

AB45051 0.20-0.30 mm Filtration Sand 50 (0.5 cubic foot) poly bags
AB10050 1/4" x 1/8" Support Gravel 4 (0.5 cubic foot) poly bags
AA21050 1/2" x 1/4" Support Gravel 4 (0.5 cubic foot) poly bags
PA11099 Pallets 1 pallet
TA12099 Shipping & Handling 1 LTL Van

WATER PURIFICATION: UV-A LIGHT DISINFECTION

Another water purification method is SODIS, or solar disinfection. The ability of UV light to kill bacteria and viruses has been known to scientists since the early 1900s. It is possible to fill a clean, transparent 1-to-2-liter PET bottle with water, expose it to the sun for at least 6 hours under a bright sky (in open air, since an enclosed car or small room might reach 185°F, the temperature at which PET bottles may leach.) In most situations the water would be safe to drink. Over four million people in the world drink SODIS treated water. As the table below indicates, since chemicals are not removed by this method, it should not be relied on if chemical contamination (arsenic, fluoride, agricultural residues) is likely to be in the water.

EFFECTIVENESS IN REMOVAL

TYPE	PROTOZOA	BACTERIA	VIRUSES	CHEMICALS	PORE SIZE
UV with pre-filtration	Very high	Very high	Very high	Not effective	NA

This method has been used and recommended by the World Health Organization for decades in poor countries. UV-A radiation is strongly reduced on cloudy days, and turbidity of the water can also protect the pathogens from UV-A radiation. The use of glass is discouraged, because whether or not it blocks UV-A radiation depends on the exact type of glass and its thickness. In any case, only low volumes with relatively low turbidity can be treated at a time, as depth also blocks penetration.

Since 1998, a large-scale UV treatment has been available for areas with electricity. Developed by Dr. Ashok Gadgil of the Lawrence Berkeley National Laboratory based on his experience in India, the system is simple, inexpensive, easy to maintain, and can produce disinfected water at the rate of 15 liters of water a minute. The manufacturer, UV Waterworks, says each unit can deliver safe drinking water for a village of 2,000 for under US$2 per person per year, including amortized capital costs. The standard unit would likely be used in our situation by a neighborhood rather than a single household, although at present the unit is affordable for many middle-class Americans.

"UV Waterworks Standard contains a germicidal ultraviolet (UV) lamp positioned over a shallow water pan. Water flows through the unit by gravity, staying in the water chamber 12 seconds to ensure adequate disinfection. No water pressure is required to operate the unit. The flow control unit is used with a clean water storage tank to limit water flow into UV Waterworks to a maximum of 4 gallons (15 liters) per minute and to mechanically shut off water flow into UV Waterworks when the tank is full and reestablish water flow as water is drawn out of the tank."[128] At the time of writing, the cost is listed as $1500 plus shipping and handling.

Water storage may enable us to stay where we are

WATER STORAGE: CISTERNS

In areas that receive rain in batches rather than with regularity, rainwater storage becomes vital—and may prove life-sustaining if community systems fail. Large cisterns are the answer when rain falls only in certain seasons, and, while they are expensive to build or buy, having one may mean the difference between remaining in that location and migrating elsewhere. Not only scarcity but also groundwater contamination due to mining or oil drilling is causing increasing numbers of households to turn to rainwater collection via roof-catchment cisterns. Further filtering is required for drinking water, using methods already mentioned. During my early childhood my mother's parents had an elevated, covered, and strained rainwater cistern next to the kitchen wall, with water piped to a faucet at the sink. The use of rainwater cisterns is an ancient practice, utilizing the same basic principles we would use today. At present, websites such as that of Penn State Extension service offer detailed, free, ready-to-print instructions.[129]

Most states have extension services that are prepared to offer help, sometimes in person, for residents needing assistance with water needs. I'm on the mailing list for several emailed newsletters that come from our extension service at North Carolina State University, and I often look on the internet to see what other states' land-grant universities advise about a question. Again I say, "Use these resources while we have them."

WATER STORAGE: RAIN BARRELS

To save the water that falls onto the roof of a home or outbuilding, rain barrels can be placed under downspouts. The water conservation website of Pender County, North Carolina, says, "Consider a roof with a surface area of 1,000 square feet. One inch of rain, running off a 1,000 square foot surface, amounts to 625 gallons of rainwater."[130]

Rain barrel with screened water intake and spigot set low.

An inexpensive rain barrel can be made from a fifty-gallon plastic outdoor garbage can with lid. One method outlined in the Notes [131] calls for the following supplies:

Brass spigot (to which you can connect a garden hose)
Watertight sealant
Teflon tape
Two rubber washers, two metal washers, and one nut
Power drill and bit
Box cutter or utility knife
Landscaping fabric or fine mesh screen
Hacksaw or other metal-cutting device

Water storage: storing water in the land, berms and swales

When we moved into the small, multi-generational home I now occupy with one of my daughters and her son, our landscaping goal was to capture on the property all of the water that falls onto it as rain. We want to have no run-off, and we're located at the highest point of a hill. To accomplish this goal, we designed a berm and swale layout in which the swales serve as the garden paths and the berms are the garden beds. The illustration below shows the profile of our front yard, which slopes downward from the house (from left to right in the drawing). There are four berms and three swales.

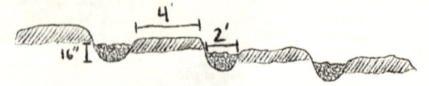

Each swale is two feet wide and sixteen inches deep. Each berm, or garden bed, is four feet wide. Water flowing down the hill is held in the swales, to be slowly released into the berms on either side.

The swales, in other words, are trenches from which soil is removed, and the berms are the raised ground formed along the ditches as the soil is transferred from ditch to bed, or swale to berm.

To encourage the capture of rainwater in the swales, we laid out the swale lines along the contour of the hill with the help of a hand-made A-frame level. As we determined the level for each portion of the length, we marked the position of the A-frame's legs with flags. The flags marked the edges of the trenches to be dug.

A-frame level
(construction directions found at location [132] in the notes)

The digging was done by hand by a strong, young neighbor. He borrowed a mattock to break up the hard-packed clay subsoil, and he piled the clay onto the four-foot spaces between swales that we had designated as beds. In order for the swale to hold water rather than send it downhill, the bottom of each trench must be quite level. The A-frame level made that possible. When it rains, the swales fill with water and hold it there until it gradually soaks into the berms, watering the roots of the plants in those beds. Last, we made paths by filling the swales with large pine bark nuggets to the height we desired, and we made planting beds by adding topsoil and other garden soil amendments to the berms. We've found that even with a great deluge—and we've had four-to six-inch rains several times since we moved here—there is no runoff into the street or the downhill yard, and in dry weather we almost never need to irrigate.

On the steeper hill that is the site of the community orchard, we hired a contractor to build much larger berms and swales with machinery. In this case we did not fill in the swales to make paths. We seeded the swales with grass and are planting the berms with fruit trees and compatible ground cover. The greater expanse allows for gentler slopes and makes the entire area walkable.

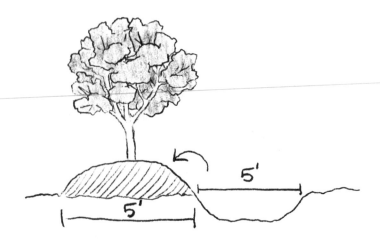

We solved a run-off problem in a similar way on the hill above the community garden, which is near the bottom of a fairly steep incline. With each heavy rain, the beds at the upper end of the garden were damaged by the force of water coming onto them from the land above. The contractor dug a ditch four feet wide and deep. We filled the ditch with old hardwood logs, scrap paper, twigs, scrap lumber (untreated), and other woody material to create a special kind of raised bed planting area. After the contractor used the machine to toss back in all the soil and clay he had removed earlier, we had a hugelkultur bed: "a centuries-old, traditional way of building a garden bed from rotten logs and plant debris. These mound shapes are created by marking out an area for a raised bed, clearing the land, and then heaping up woody material (ideally already partially rotted) topped with compost and soil."[133]

Hugelkultur doesn't require a ditch—the woody material will soak up water when placed on the surface, too—but the depth allowed us to capture a greater amount of water as it came down the hill. This bed, like the ones in our yard and the swales in the orchard, was laid out on the contour of the incline by means of the A-frame level.

Ordinarily hugelkultur, pronounced hoo-gul-culture, which means hill culture or hill mound, is simply a no-dig raised bed created over a layer of wood material. It holds moisture well, builds fertility, and expands the planting space in a given area. The gradual decay of wood is a consistent source of long-term nutrients; a large bed might give out a constant supply of nutrients for twenty years or more if you use only hardwoods. The composting wood also generates heat, which should extend the growing season. Soil aeration increases as those branches and logs break down, and since the logs and branches act like a sponge, rainwater is stored and then released during drier times.[134] Avoid using wood from black locust (it will not decompose), black walnut (it bears the juglone toxin), or old growth redwood (heartwood will not decompose and redwood compost can prevent seed germination).

WATER STORAGE: STORING WATER IN THE LAND, KEYLINE

From Australia has come yet another means of holding water in the land: the key line method developed by mining geologist and engineer P. A. Yeomans. "The central idea behind 'Keyline' water management is to consciously slow, sink and spread rainwater by relieving compaction, opening up pore space in compacted soil and distributing excess water towards drier parts of the landscape. This has the effect of buffering the natural concentration of water towards valleys and reducing flooding. By maximizing the flow of water to drier ridges (using precise plow lines or mounds that fall slightly off contour), the method infiltrates it across the broadest possible area. Only the keyline is purely *on contour*. The other parallel lines encourage water to shed towards the ridges."[135] The parallel lines are created by a special plow that penetrates the subsoil to a depth of two inches below existing rooting depth without inverting the soil.

One of my friends has adapted this large-scale agricultural technique for water storage for use on her city lot. The next four paragraphs are the description I asked her to write for this section of the handbook.

> The "Australian method for gardens" is modeled on the Australian method for farms. Ken B. Yeomans, son of P.A., made an anthology of his father's articles in *Water for Every Farm*.[136] In order to avoid duplication from the multiple articles, he chopped out the duplications and pieced together the rest, making the text hard to follow in some sections. A more current version of the Yeomans method for farms is at this link,[137] but the book does have information that isn't on the website. I suggest reading the website first, and then going to the book.
>
> Before you start on the Australian method for your garden, clean and sharpen the cutting edge of your shovel. Your work will go a lot easier with a clean and sharp shovel. The most efficient shovel for this method is one with a square blade, but if your soil is too stiff for that, then use a shovel with a pointed blade. Start by going out in the area that you're going to prepare for your garden, and step on the shovel enough to push the cutting edge of the blade in the soil, vertically, about two inches. (It is the blade that's vertical; the shaft and handle of the blade may tip forward or back.)
>
> Now, without pulling the blade of the shovel out of the ground, tip the handle back, slowly, so the cutting edge of the blade is pushing the ground in front of the blade forward. Eventually the ground will "give" or "pop," and that ground will feel spongy if you step on it. The ground now has lots of cracks, which are good for water retention, earthworm wanderings, and roots. Next measure how far ahead of the blade the ground is spongy, and start popping the soil like that, with the blade that distance from the front of the garden bed, across the whole front of the bed. Then come back and do that again, "row by row" until you put in the row across the back of the bed. Now, water the bed gently, to start water working into all those cracks. If you stop now, you already have done a lot to make your garden soil more fertile.
>
> But you can also do more: The next thing you can do is put down a little bit of topsoil or compost, and rake it along the bed, so it catches a little bit in the spongy soil. And water gently again. Now sow clover in

the bed, and as the clover grows, water it. When the clover is just about to start making buds, mow it. Clover roots pull in a lot of nitrogen, and you now have nitrogen fertilizer down in your garden bed. (If you let the buds form before you mow; the buds will pull nitrogen and other nutrients up from the roots into the buds and you'll lose those nutrients from the soil.) You don't need to bring in earthworms. If you build it, they will come.

In order to capture the water that comes onto your property, whether by precipitation or run-off from someone else's land or driveway, you can follow the same technique throughout your property, not just where you have garden beds. My bias is to have garden beds everywhere, filled with vegetables, fruits, medicinal and culinary herbs, pollinator flowers, and plants grown only to beautify and sweeten the world, such as peonies, lilacs, and fancy irises. If you want an area of grass for children, or as a playing field for adult sports, then treat it as my friend, using her Australian method, suggests treating a garden bed. View the grass as a garden, too, and as a feature of your water management strategy. In the future, a conventional grass lawn will be an indicator of the kind of indifference to nature that has brought us into peril. Nature requires a high level of diversity in plant life to support a high level of health for the insects and animals that depend on plants to survive.

Nature also works to protect the moisture in soil from evaporation. With the increased evaporative demand (a term describing the atmosphere's capacity to pull moisture from the ground) being observed with climate change, covering the ground as thickly as possible, with either plants or mulch, becomes a first-line defense against water loss.[138] No bare soil!

Water conservation plays a large role in water provisioning

Most of us can manage with less water than we've habitually used in times of water abundance. Americans are said to use an average of 82 gallons of water a day at home.[139] Remember the story about Saturday night baths in pioneer days? First the papa bathed in the tub, then the children, then the mama, and last the baby, and "don't throw the baby out with the bath water!" As a child who grew up with well water, I learned to notice when the water was turned on, and the sound of water running into a sink can still make me anxious. I bless those faucets in public restrooms that cut off when hands move away. "Shorter showers "and water-saving showerheads have been common recommendations among conservation-minded people throughout my adulthood.

Below I offer suggestions for using less water in ordinary household routines. Such lists are already easy to find, and as drought becomes an increasing burden of the American West, expect national publications to carry more such lists. Pender County in North Carolina has posted sensible home water conservation guidelines.[140] Several of the suggestions below were posted online in 2018 when Cape Town was running out of water, by a food writer in that area.[141] Other ideas were gathered by asking acquaintances how they saved water. Many are the old "reduce, reuse, recycle" plan applied to this situation.

1. Fix leaky faucets, plumbing joints, and toilets.

2. Don't let the water run while brushing teeth, shaving, or washing hands or face. Save water and energy by washing hands with soap and cold water instead of turning on the hot water and waiting for it to run hot.

3. Lower the setting on your hot water heater. You won't have to mix it with cold water in order to use it.

4. Flush less often: According to the US Geological Survey's Water Science School report of June 20, 2019, the largest use of household water is to flush the toilet. "When it's yellow, let it mellow."

5. Learn to cook without water. This is when grilling, frying, baking, roasting, and broiling come to the front of the line.

6. Pasta and rice can be water wasters—except for dishes like lasagna and cannelloni, in which the pasta is softened by tomato sauce and doesn't require pre-boiling. With rice, try recipes that incorporate the water in the dish like a pilaf or risotto.

7. Use a steamer basket with vegetables like beets, carrots, and potatoes. Vegetables cook as quickly in steam, and only a little water is needed in the bottom of the pan.

8. A baked casserole might stay moist due to the moisture in the vegetables: potatoes, then onions, then green peas. Cover and cook at a low temperature.

9. Wash dishes in water that was first used to rinse vegetables. Or use greywater from the laundry to wash dishes, then rinse with fresh water at boiling temperature.

10. Rinse dishes in a pan, not under the running tap. Using the least amount of detergent necessary minimizes the rinse water needed.
11. Keep a large jar or bucket on the kitchen counter to receive rinsing or cooking water. Use it for watering plants, for thawing frozen food, or for especially dirty cleanup jobs.

If we count the water usage of the power plants that create our electricity, the amount is significantly more than the 82 gallons daily per person the US Geological Survey reports. The average per person for our total water usage of thermoelectric power plants—coal, oil, natural gas and nuclear—for the year 2015 was 415 gallons each day. (US electricity-generating power plants used 133,000,000,000 gallons per day in 2015, and the total population of the United States for that year was 320,090,857.)[142]

In addition to our water usage via electricity, our individual share of the water consumption of other industries must weigh into the picture. The Environmental Protection Agency (EPA) estimates US industrial processes require more than 18.2 billion gallons per day—that's 18,200,000,000 gallons—drawn directly from a water source such as a river, not including water use from a public water supply.[143] The industrial way of life is water-intensive, yet another reason not to lament too strongly its passing. We can hope for at least this advantage during blackouts and as factories shut down: that there may be a higher percentage of fresh water available for people to drink, and maybe rivers, streams, and lakes will also be cleaner.

The United Nations publication "The Human Right to Water and Sanitation" states the need for water as between 50 and 100 liters per person per day. Fifty liters is about thirteen gallons, or two and a half five-gallon buckets. According to the World Health Organization (WHO), this is the amount needed to ensure that most basic needs are met and few health concerns arise.[144] UNICEF estimates that over two billion people live in countries where water supply is inadequate now, and that with climate change half of the world's population could be living in areas facing water scarcity by 2025.[145] We can hope that first-world industries located in those countries where 50 liters is not currently available will also shut down, and that water will be freed up toward that need.

Additional resources

The Biosand Booklet, a project of the University of South Florida College of Education, College of Engineering, and Patel College of Global Sustainability. https://www.usf.edu/nsf-ires/documents/mccannprojectsupplementary/bsf-booklet.pdf.

Aric McBay, *Peak Oil Survival* (Guilford CT: The Lyons Press, 2006). The book offers a full list of water possibilities for people without the services of a community system. In the 39 pages that address water projects, McBay gives clear advice about obtaining groundwater by means of wells and springs; collecting rainwater; utilizing surface water; and obtaining small amounts of water for survival, such as from soil and plants. He also discusses water treatment, disinfection and filtering, and the use of grey water. This carefully researched and accessible manual also refers readers to sources of additional information. In addition to the pages on meeting water needs, he offers helpful information about cooling, heating, and lighting.

Laura Allen, *The Water-Wise Home: How to Conserve, Capture, and Reuse Water in Your Home and Landscape* (North Adams MA: Storey Press, 2015). Ideas and instructions for building systems that conserve and reuse water in the home and garden.

Laura Allen, *Greywater, Green Landscape: How to Install Simple Water-Saving Irrigation Systems in Your Yard* (North Adams MA: Storey Press, 2017). Primarily for those who have piped-in water from community systems, this empowering manual offers practical strategies for water management, do-it-yourself instructions, and step-by-step photography for constructing and installing water-saving techniques. Be aware that the piping of greywater is currently illegal in most places.

P.A. Yeomans, *Water for Every Farm: Yeomans Keyline Plan* (South Australia: Griffin Press Ltd., 1993).

HOW WILL WE PROVIDE FOR SAFE SANITATION?

Sanitation is closely linked with water, and in US urban settings it is tied to reliable community services. A breakdown in these systems is a frightening prospect if our homes are connected to the pipes of municipal water and sewer provisioning. I received a glimpse of the disorder and distress that might follow by reading about a North Carolina community that suffered a broken sewer system.

Residents of the Eagle Creek subdivision had been dealing with outages and disruptions in their sewage system occasionally for twenty years, but problems became acute in late 2020. A November 2021 news story relates that the intricate maze of pumps and pipes and pits had failed for the fourth consecutive day, "funneling sewage into people's toilets and showers. To keep their homes from becoming cesspools, owners had no choice but to open their cleanout valves and allow the sewage to escape. 'On Halloween night people were peeing in their yards because they couldn't flush their toilets,' one neighbor said. 'People were saying it smells like a zoo.' The stench was wafting from raw sewage that had ponded in the roadside ditches."[146]

People in cities and suburbs need to prepare in advance to take charge should services fail. Eagle Creek seems to have been victimized by poor management on the part of a private company. Public water-sewage utilities are also vulnerable to poor management and will be increasingly less able to handle waste reliably as economic conditions deteriorate. The more intense rainfall events of climate change pose an additional problem. Sewer systems in many cities, stressed by age and growing populations, will spew more raw refuse into the streets during heavy rains. The amount of stormwater entering a combined sewer system can be overwhelming for the pipes and the treatment plant, leading to combined sewer overflows that either pollute rivers and streams or release raw sewage into nearby communities, or both.[147]

When I visited rural relatives and friends in my childhood, they had no intricate maze of pumps and pipes and pits serving their bathrooms. Instead they used outhouses for toilet purposes, sitting on wooden seats set either over pits, or on planks with holes that dumped excrement directly onto the ground, to be carried away or covered every day with soil and/or lime.

If the time comes when community water-sewer services aren't available, we won't have to return to those practices. With proper preparation we should be able to keep indoor convenience, although with a step up in responsibility. Healthy bodies defecate, and we might as well accept our role in the nutrient cycle—grow food, eat, defecate, process organic matter and return to the soil, grow food, eat, defecate, return to soil—rather than resenting it. With a little bit of knowledge about sanitation procedures, we can work with nature to handle this part of being human with grace and skill. In that spirit, let's talk about our options.

How will we dispose of sewage: Managing septic tanks

It would be possible for people who have enough land at their disposal to put in septic tanks for sewage, and to use water-filled toilets just as residents of many unincorporated areas in the United States do now—if they have a good supply of water to pipe into the house. A conventional system consists of a septic tank and a drain field. The septic tank breaks down organic matter and separates out the oil, grease, and solids. Heavy solids settle to the bottom of the tank while greases and lighter solids float to the top. The solids stay in the tank while the wastewater is discharged into a series of underground perforated pipes that allow the liquid to slowly drain into the soil of the drain field. In a properly functioning septic system, percolation through the soil removes harmful bacteria and nutrients. These conventional gravel/stone systems have been used for decades, but they take a lot of space. A more compact system uses pre-formed plastic chambers buried in an earthen trench. Wastewater is delivered to the top of each chamber by a solid plastic pipe. Effluent seeps into soil across the bottom of the chamber, where soil microbes treat it.

In addition to the time, effort, and expense of installation, the tanks of either system need to be cleaned out periodically, and the ground above a septic field requires special management. Only shallow-rooted, drought-tolerant plants can grow there, because plant roots could clog the drainpipes and potentially damage the drain field. Since excess water slows down or stops the wastewater treatment process, roof drains should be directed elsewhere, and extra watering should be avoided. Detergents may increase the soil pH and effluent may increase its salinity. Raised beds can't be created over the drainage area because the added soil depth would interfere with proper evaporation, and even if such beds are elevated, their weight is likely to damage the tank or compact the soil, causing the wastewater to go back into the house. It goes without saying that driveways and parking pads can't be placed over the drain field.[148]

How will we dispose of sewage: composting human excrement

For most of us, therefore, a septic field, even if we felt able to manage that technology, would require space we don't have, or don't want to devote to that purpose. Fortunately there is a simpler though less familiar way to manage toilet needs: let nature's decomposition agents do it by means of compost. We've already talked about the work of microorganisms to help with food growing and with water purification. In the section on biosand filtration of water, we saw that the top layer of a biosand filter contains microorganisms that purify incoming water. In the section on food growing, they were mentioned as soil agents and factors in simple composting. These natural technologies depend upon the functions of tiny creatures who are far more essential to life on Earth than we are. Like the bacteria in and on our bodies, they are the sanitation engineers of the biosystem. They maintain the health of living creatures by overpowering microorganisms whose agenda is less friendly to humans.

If, like me, you have questioned the wisdom of defecating into drinking-quality water, composting may be a welcome possibility. As Brian Barth has written on Modern Farmer website, "The gleaming white commode, a mainstay of modern civilization, is not something most folks question. But anyone who does stop to ponder why we flush our feces and urine into nearby streams and rivers (albeit via a wastewater treatment plant) quickly sees that this is a rather daft arrangement. Human waste, just like manure from farm animals, is high in nutrients and organic matter. Flushing the toilet isn't just a waste of waste. It's pollution. Why not recycle it as fertilizer?"[149]

If we don't want to compost our excrement, we can use one of the dry toilet systems now widely available—if we have a vendor who will go around the area collecting the filled buckets and taking the contents away, perhaps to be recycled as fertilizer. These systems include chemical toilets, urine-diverting toilets, and eco-toilets, to name a few that are now on the market.

But if we want to keep the fertilizer for our own garden use, we can adopt Joseph Jenkins's "humanure" composting strategy. I'm all for doing that, now that I know I won't have deal with more mess than with a baby's diapers. Once I had read *The Humanure Handbook*, I was more than interested—at least in theory—for I admit I haven't put the concept into practice yet. I've begun scouting for materials, though, and am deciding on the best place to site the compost.

With the style of compost toilet Jenkins recommends, the composting takes place after the bucket part of the toilet is taken outdoors and the contents are added to a properly prepared compost pile. Kept at the internal temperatures of 113°F to 160°F in which mesophilic bacteria thrive, the resulting compost is safe enough to nourish food crops. "Mesophilic" refers to bacteria that do well in moderate temperatures.

I will quote extensively here from Jenkins's book. You might say that Joseph Jenkins is the author of this next section of the handbook. Because the information I sought was scattered throughout the book, I'm rearranging it to present in a step-by-step-order. The page numbers found in the notes will lead you to the discussion of each topic in the book.

I will outline here the method he recommends from toilet to compost, and I'll share his answers to the other questions I had when I started the investigation. But I encourage you to order the book and read it for yourself. Google Books says, "This is the 4th edition of a self-published book that no respectable publisher would touch with a ten-foot shovel. The 1st edition was published in 1994 with a print run of 600 copies, which the author expected to watch decompose in his garage for the rest of his life. Now, 24 years later, the book has sold over 65,000 print copies in the US alone, been translated in whole or in part into 19 languages and been published in foreign editions on four continents." A used book can be purchased, but don't expect it to be cheap; the book is much in demand.

The following instructions are primarily his words. Jenkins lists four requirements: (1) the cover material (2) the toilet (3) the compost bins and (4) human management.

THE FOUR BASIC REQUIREMENTS: #1 THE COVER MATERIAL

The cover material for inside the toilet (sometimes called a loo). "For a compost toilet to function, you need a carbon-based cover material . . . a fine material that has a small degree of residual moisture. . . . It must be a plant cellulose material." He lists sugarcane bagasse (what's left after crushing sugarcane) and rice husks or hulls for people in some locations, but says sawdust from trees, with residual moisture, is "perfect." Not wood chips or wood shavings. "The residual moisture is what makes it an effective biofilter. Bacteria live in the biofilms coating the wood particles. If you're using bone-dry sawdust as a cover material and you notice odor escaping from the toilet, mist the cover material with water when you're adding it. . . . It's the cover material that eliminates the need for venting. When you're using appropriate cover material, a standard toilet seat lid (other than the cover material) is all that is required to cover the toilet contents. The loo receptacle never needs its own separate lid until it's removed from the loo cabinet."[150]

The cover material for the compost pile. "On the other hand, the cover materials used on the compost pile don't have to be in fine particles and can be either dry or moist. Straw, hay, grasses, weeds, leaves—anything from a plant source that is clean and doesn't smell bad. Cover materials help keep your pile aerobic by creating tiny interstitial air spaces in the compost. That's all the oxygen your compost will need. . . . Always cover the contents thoroughly. If you smell odors, add more cover material. . . . Add cover material until it doesn't."[151]

THE FOUR BASIC REQUIREMENTS: #2 THE COMPOST TOILET

"The toilet must have receptacles that are sturdy, waterproof, and durable. If you're emptying receptacles by hand, they must be small enough to be handled by one or two people. . . . If you're alone and five gallons is too much, empty the receptacle when it's half full. . . . All urine, fecal material, and toilet paper go into the loo, as does anything else that would normally go into a flush toilet. You can also throw in the cardboard tubes from the center of toilet paper rolls. You can vomit in the toilet. Just don't put food scraps because you can risk a fruit fly infestation. You can put food scraps in the receptacle after the receptacle has been removed from the toilet housing, and a lid has been placed on it. It's all going to the same compost pile anyway. . . . You can make your own loo for very little money out of scrap wood, and you can find recycled plastic receptacles available cheap or free. You should construct the loo to fit the receptacles, so make sure you have several receptacles that are exactly the same size . . . with tight-fitting lids."[152]

THE FOUR BASIC REQUIREMENTS: #3 THE COMPOST BINS

"You will need at least two, one to fill until full and another to fill while the first one cures or ages. The purpose of the bin is to contain the organic material vertically above ground in such a manner that dogs, goats, horses, and other critters won't be able to get into it."[153] "You may need to line it with wire mesh if you live in a rat-infested area."[154] If needed, you can lay wire fencing over the top of the pile for further protection.

"Size the bins so it takes a year to fill them. If you're a larger group, you may need several bins or larger bins. A standard family bin size is roughly five feet square and four feet high. Position the bins on soil, not on concrete. . . . The soil interface is important for several reasons. It provides a biological conduit for micro- and macro-organisms to enter and exit the compost pile. It also provides an area for compost microbes to reside after the bin is emptied; these microbes help inoculate the next pile. The upper few inches of soil also act as a buffer for excess liquid, absorbing it when needed. . . . Always dish the soil base to create a bowl underneath the compost pile. Take the dirt you dig out—and it doesn't need to be much—and throw it up against the inside of the bin walls around the bottom edges. You now have a shallow depression under your bin providing extra insurance against any leachate seeping out the bottom.

"Before adding any toilet material to your bin, first lay a 'biological sponge' in the bottom. This is a cushion of grasses, weeds, leaves, hay, straw, or whatever else you have on hand and whatever you're using for cover material, at least 18 inches or more. Thicker is fine; it will compress down and disappear in the finished compost. Put enough of a biological sponge in the bottom so that you can open a hole in (the center of) it to place your first organic deposit, then rake the sponge material back over the deposit and add cover material. The fresh deposit, which may be toilet material, is now buried in the cover material. Add more cover material. Don't let your compost pile become shaped like the Matterhorn—keep it flattened.

"Always keep a compost thermometer in the center of your active pile. Twenty-inch thermometers are inexpensive, and they give you a constant reading, letting you know what's going on in your pile."[155] "Typical temperatures range from 110°F (43°C) to 130°F (54°C). . . .

For some reason, the compost seems to stay around 120ºF most of the summer months at a depth of twenty inches. . . . If you don't feed it the temperature will drop. . . . If you feed it, the temperature will rise again."[156]

"Pull the thermometer out before adding new material. By adding incoming material into the center of the compost pile, you achieve some important things: you inject the new material into the most active part of the pile; you cover it thoroughly, not only with cover material, but also with existing compost; and you create a cover material cushion around the *outer edges* of the compost, thereby enveloping the compost in cover material, like a blanket. This insulates the pile, keeps the outside edges of the compost from cooling down, and keeps compost from falling out of any gaps in the bin walls, such as happens with pallet bins. By using a cover material cushion *around* your compost, you can use any kind of bin: wood, block, brick, metal, or plastic, and holes, spaces, or gaps are not needed in the side walls for aeration."[157]

THE FOUR BASIC REQUIREMENTS: #4 HUMAN MANAGEMENT

"The final *necessary* element in a compost toilet system is human management. . . . You, or someone, must take responsibility for the compost toilet you're using. A compost toilet system will quickly fail if managed poorly."[158]

After learning these steps, I still had seven important questions to ask Jenkins about the humanure project.

QUESTION #1 WHAT CAN BE COMPOSTED?

"Anything on Earth that had been alive, or from a living thing, such as manure, plants, leaves, sawdust, peat, straw, grass clippings, food scraps, and urine; and anything that will rot, such as cotton clothing, wool rugs, rags, paper, animal carcasses, junk mail, and cardboard." But "wood chips don't compost well at all unless they're ground into sawdust. . . . Never put woody-stemmed plants, such as tree saplings, in your compost pile."[159] Some materials such as bone, hair, and eggshells don't decompose well, but they do no harm.

QUESTION #2 WHAT KIND OF PILE?

Above ground, contained, and covered. "A contained pile (versus an open pile or windrow) keeps the material from drying out or cooling down prematurely. Bins, as opposed to open piles, also keep out nuisance animals. . . . A bin doesn't have to cost money; it can be made from recycled wood, cement blocks, hay bales, repurposed pallets, or whatever else is at hand. . . . When a fresh deposit is added to the compost pile, especially a smelly deposit, it's essential to cover it with clean organic material to eliminate odors and to prevent flies from being attracted to the compost."

QUESTION #3 HOW MOIST DOES THE PILE NEED TO BE KEPT?

"A dry pile will just sit there looking bored. . . . Microorganisms don't walk—they swim. They don't have legs like land animals do, and they need moisture for motility. Microbes live in biofilms coating the particles and surfaces. . . . The water required for compost-making may be around two hundred to three hundred gallons for each cubic yard of finished compost. This moisture requirement can be met when human urine is used in the compost and the pile is receiving adequate rainfall. Additional water can come from moist organic materials such as food scraps. . . . In a desert situation, watering will likely be necessary to produce a moisture content equivalent to a squeezed-out sponge. . . . Lately I've been collecting discarded beer from a local brewery in five-gallon buckets and pouring it over the compost piles. The piles love it. . . . Aerobic bacteria will suffer from a lack of oxygen if drowned in liquid, which would occur, for example, at the bottom of a pit in standing water."[160]

QUESTION #4 HOW IS THE PILE AERATED?

"Oxygen is necessary for aerobic compost, and there are numerous ways to aerate a compost pile." When a compost pile is properly constructed, no additional aeration will be needed. . . . Build the pile in a constructed bin above ground allowing tiny interstitial air spaces to be trapped in the compost. This is done by using materials in the compost such as hay, straw, weeds, and the like.[161]

QUESTION #5 DOES THE PILE NEED TO BE TURNED?

"If it's above ground and not underwater, the organic mass will be aerobic. No forced aeration will be needed, and no poking, prodding, digging, or turning whatsoever is required. . . . The more frequently compost piles are turned, the more agricultural nutrients they lose. . . . Turning compost piles in cold climates can also cause them to lose too much heat. In fact, what's the point of diminishing the heat of the pile, no matter what the climate? That's what turning the pile does.... Those volatile fatty acids, ketones, terpenes, aldehydes, alcohols, ammonia, bacteria, fungi, viruses, allergens, endotoxins, antigens, various toxins, glucans, mold components, pollen, plant fibers, and so on that are inside the compost pile belong inside the compost pile. What's the point of releasing them into the air?... I can assure you that if you're composting material from toilets, you don't want to be turning the pile if you don't have to."[162]

QUESTION #6 IS IT LEGAL?

"Both backyard composting and farm composting are generally exempt from regulations unless the compost is being sold, or removed from the property on which it is made, or the compost operation is large. The National Sanitation Foundation has nothing to do with composting. Composting is not a wastewater treatment system and is not subject to the regulations that govern such systems.... Dry toilets that dehydrate and degrade the organic material inside them, producing septage, are regulated in many states. A humanure toilet does not degrade organic material; it simply collects it.[163]

"What about 'health agents'? Health authorities can be led by misinformation.... Therefore, if you are using a compost toilet and are having a problem with any authority, we will donate, free of charge, a copy of *The Humanure Handbook*, fourth edition, to any permitting agent or health authority.... Well-informed health professionals and environmental authorities are aware that 'human waste' presents an environmental dilemma that is not going away."[164]

QUESTION #7 HOW SAFE IS THE COMPOST FROM A PROPERLY MANAGED COMPOST TOILET SYSTEM?

Jenkins's big DON'Ts concern safety: "(1) never allow human excrement to come into contact with water; (2) never allow human excrement to come into contact with soil.

"What's wrong with soil? ... The answer, in a word, is parasites. Some intestinal parasites coevolved with humans over millennia simply because we have the habit of defecating on soil. Several human intestinal parasites therefore evolved requiring a period in soil during their life cycle. When we're allowing human excrement to come into contact with soil, we're enabling these parasites to multiply. For example, roundworms (*Ascaris lumbricoides*) do not multiply in the human host;

instead, eggs are excreted in feces, allowing the larval stage to develop *in soil*. . . . People ingest infective eggs by putting their dirty fingers in their mouths"or on food which they then eat. Hence Jenkins's third "rule of sanitation: (3) wash your hands after defecating."[165]

"Two primary factors lead to the death of pathogens in humanure. The first is temperature. A compost pile that is properly managed will destroy pathogens with the heat and biological activity it generates. . . . A thermophilic compost pile will destroy pathogens, including worm eggs. . . . One need not strive for extremely high temperature in a compost pile to feel confident about the destruction of pathogens. It may be more realistic to maintain lower temperature in a compost pile for longer periods of time, such as 122°F (50°C) for twenty-four hours, or 115°F (46°C) for a week.

"The second factor is time. Given enough time, the wide biodiversity of microorganisms in the compost will destroy pathogens by the antagonism, competition, consumption, and antibiotic inhibitors provided by the beneficial microorganisms. Feachem et al. state that three months retention time will kill all the pathogens in a dry toilet except worm eggs."[166] "The septage obtained from these types of toilets can theoretically be composted again in a thermophilic pile and rendered suitable for food gardens. Otherwise, the septage can be moved to an outdoor compost bin and left to age for an additional year or two."[167]

"If you're composting humanure from a population with endemic diseases, an additional year-long curing period should be considered. This will require additional compost bins. In that situation, after a bin is filled it is left to rest for two years. If in doubt about the hygienic safety of any compost, either test it for pathogens in a laboratory, or use it agriculturally where it will not come in contact with food crops, and wear gloves when handling it."[168]

"Humanure is not any more dangerous than the body from which it is excreted. The danger lies in what we do with the excrement, not in the material itself."[169]

Jenkins elaborates on all these points, and you will want to read his chatty comments as well as the abundant research he offers, some of which he used in the writing of his PhD dissertation, which was the backbone of the first edition.

A HUMANURE TESTIMONY

In *Compost Everything: The Good Guide to Extreme Composting*, David the Good writes, "Are you prepared to deal with sewage in a crisis? . . . A few years ago my wife and I actually did an experiment to see if we would be ready for the septic side of a collapse situation (yes, this is what we do with our spare time). I built a five-gallon bucket toilet based on the plans in Joseph Jenkins's *Humanure Handbook*, then installed it in the bathroom of our little 3/1 house in Tennessee. For an entire year my family used that toilet and I hauled buckets out of the house in all kinds of weather to a big compost pile at the back of our property. There I'd set up a washing station in the bushes so I could sterilize the buckets after emptying them. Keep in mind that this was a suburban neighborhood. If this system had stunk at all or attracted flies, etc., we would have been discovered. There wasn't even a fence around my back yard. . . . We composted a year's worth of 'waste,' then used that compost a year later for our gardening. No one got sick. No one had a problem. No neighbors complained. That was because we did it right by following the Jenkins system carefully."[170]

How will we dispose of potentially dangerous trash: "Compost everything"

I'm thinking that as public services decline, we'll have responsibility for disposing of more things than our excrement. In the old days every large property had a burn barrel, most commonly a large metal can that previously had held fuel oil. Once or twice a year residents filled it with everything that would burn, set it afire, and blew smoke with unidentified particulate matter all over the area. In dry seasons burning was forbidden, punishable by fines, and frowned on to the point that law-abiding people didn't do it. We know more about air quality now and have reason to avoid making more air pollution than might be necessary for winter warmth. Earth-wise people will learn to make hot or slow-cooking compost for most formerly-burned trash—and also make less smoke even for winter heating.

But how do we dispose of things in the category David the Good calls "highly nitrogenous, potentially dangerous, stinky, yet mineral-rich materials?" Jenkins says the compost piles he creates will handle the bodies of small animals, and David the Good offers another way of composting. He creates what he calls "melon pits."

1) "Dig a two to three foot deep hole. . . . Make sure the depth is sufficiently discouraging to animals. It's also important to make sure the contents are far enough below the natural soil line that they don't end up getting washed out in a heavy rain.
2) "Dump in chunks of wood and sticks. Bigger chunks are better. Again, this is for water retention. They'll hold water for years as well as provide a slow release of nutrition." He cautions that wood chips require supplemental nitrogen if plants are to be grown in that soil.
3) "Dump in dangerous and gross stuff. This can be almost anything you can imagine. I've buried a dead rooster, baked beans, rotten eggs, and even a human placenta. Crazy? No, I did it for science!
4) "Cover with loose soil. Depending on your native soil conditions you can either indent your melon pit or let it become a traditional mound. Six to twelve inches of dirt over the top is usually enough to deter roving animals. . . . Adding a few inches of mulch isn't a bad idea.
5) "Plant (and stand back). Sprawling vines work the best with this method." He mentions squash and melons—hence the name "melon pit."[171]

How will we dispose of potentially dangerous trash: non-biodegradable waste

In my childhood, when household items made of metal and glass outwore their usefulness, people dropped them into ravines or onto unclaimed (or uninspected) land. These informal dumps looked unsightly, but they were composed of materials less toxic than many for which we will need to find a post-life place in a post-industrial era. I'm thinking especially of plastics.

If community waste disposal trucks stop coming by and dumpsters disappear, how will we dispose of plastic? Incineration is not an option, as the burning of plastics releases into the atmosphere toxic gases like dioxins, furans, mercury, and polychlorinated biphenyls (better known as PCBs). It would be helpful if manufacturers expanded recycling by reclaiming plastic waste and turning it into products like clothing, toys, tableware, and shoes, but at the moment it is cheaper for them to use oil to make new products. All over the world, however, people are recognizing the seriousness of the plastic waste problem. It has become an environmental issue of great concern.

Solutions are being pursued. Scientists are identifying bacteria and bugs that consume plastic trash. *Ideonella sakaiensis* is a bacterium from the genus Ideonella and family *Comamonadaceae* that will break down and consume the polyethylene terephthalate (PET).[172] The larvae of the darkling beetle *Zophobas morio* can survive on polystyrene, commonly called styrofoam.[173] Enzymes that rapidly break down plastic bags have been discovered in the saliva of wax worms, which are moth larvae that infest beehives.[174] Scientists are also engineering enzymes to recycle plastic.[175] In a few more years, these discoveries and innovations may become accessible.

Small-scale recycling solutions for plastics are slowly appearing as well, and given enough time with stable conditions, some that are now in isolated locations may begin to appear more widely. At present, however, we have no safe means of final disposal for anything made from plastic, and the moment when a plastic object begins to break down into pieces is the most dangerous stage for the material. The nanoplastics that result from the degrading of plastic are a severe threat to all living things.[176]

The best solution, of course, is not to bring plastic home—not to buy plastic items or items packaged with plastic. Zero-waste initiatives focus on this option, and while we can reduce the amount we purchase, removing it from our lives at this point is not possible. I can only recommend: buy as little plastic as possible, and then use, reuse, and reuse a plastic object until it begins to come apart.

At that point, when we've done our best to put every scrap to a second use and even those second-use items are collapsing, community landfills seem our best option— for as long as we have access to them. When we don't, I guess we'll have to find a place to bury it ourselves. Maybe every property should have a "plastic pit:" a deep hole ready to receive the disintegrating fragments of plastic relics. These pits would need a cover too heavy or too well protected for one person to accidentally or easily lift, and a sign in three languages indicating "Dangerous material!"

How will we keep clean in post-industrial conditions?

Of course, sanitation involves more than safe disposal. It includes all the ways we keep our bodies and our belongings, including our area of residence, clean. What we're aiming for is safety. If medical services become less available, sanitation of the right kind will become more essential than it is now. An economic crisis is commonly followed by an increase in illness, including more communicable disease. Warmer temperatures will bring new hazards as well. I think handwashing and mask wearing, as well as measures that give protection from disease-carrying insects, may be increasingly part of this picture. Even so, I hope by now you have taken into your knowledge base the understanding that microorganisms are mostly supportive of good health, which is the objective of cleanliness.

The wellness of human bodies and human habitats depends on the wellness of these beneficial unseen allies, and if in the future ordinary humans are more in control of their environments than industry is, perhaps we can create spaces that support all forms of life, including the microscopic. That would include the use of cleaning supplies that don't kill bacteria while they are removing spots.

Yet when I searched for "healthy cleaning products" on the internet, Clorox was the first hit. "Kills 99.9% of Bacteria & Viruses," the ad says. Industrial culture pairs "clean" with "sterile." There are times when we do need sterile conditions, of course, but I suggest we get our minds around a more nature-aligned vision of sanitation. As Dimitri Orlov writes, looking at us from his Russian background, "Americans consider body odors and animal smells repulsive, but acrid, toxic chemical odors (be they from deodorants and disinfectants, engine exhaust, or off gassing plastics and synthetic fabrics) are just fine, although it is the latter that are likely to kill you."[177]

I'm beginning to realize we'll be even more in need of the help of beneficial microbes as years go by. Even now the antibiotic problem—bacterial resistance—is a major medical dilemma on the edge of catastrophe. Stephen Harrod Buhner has been explaining the problem in his books. "As soon as a bacterium encounters an antibiotic, it begins to generate possible responses. This takes time, usually bacterial generations. But bacteria live a lot more quickly than we do; a new generation occurs every twenty minutes in many species."[178] As he also points out, however, we're fortunate that they are so resilient. If bacteria had not been successful in evolving resistance strategies, by this date all life on Earth would have ended.

Fighting bacteria by the methods of modern medicine is a losing proposition, and antibiotics bring harm as well as good. As these drugs get into the water and soil by means such as animal excrement, including from humans, they are destroying the biome of the ecosystem—that's what anti-life strategies do. Buhner and other herbalists study and practice with the aim of replacing dangerous, anti-life drugs with plant medicines, and we need to be sure our sanitation measures likewise support life rather than destroy it.

In *The Encyclopedia of Country Living*, Carla Emery passes on to present-day readers an article on less toxic household cleaners by Rodney Merrill. It appeared in *Backwoods Home Magazine* in 1991. Merrill lists several familiar products:

1. **Ammonia.** "This is ammonium hydroxide dissolved in water, a natural grease cutter. As long as you provide plenty of ventilation and never combine it with other chemical cleaners, ammonia is safe to use."
2. **Baking soda.** "Sodium bicarbonate is a good deodorizer and mild abrasive."
3. **Laundry bleach.** "This bleach is 5% sodium hypochlorite no matter whose name is on the label. It's an oxidizer and a natural germ killer. Chlorine bleach, as it is commonly called, is an excellent disinfectant and cleaner, and it's a powerful bacteriostatic for drinking water. Bleach plays an important role in halting the spread of contagious diseases. The trouble is, once chlorine enters lakes and streams, it combines with organic matter to create cancer-causing agents known as trihalomethanes. Therefore the general rule for chlorine bleach should be when a powerful disinfectant is crucial, use chlorine bleach—but only then."
4. **Borax.** "Borax is sodium borate. It is a good phosphate-free water softener and makes an effective but mild abrasive when used damp or dry. Caution: do not drink water that contains borax. It is toxic."
5. **Distilled white vinegar.** "Vinegar is just about the most natural substance you can find. The active cleaning ingredient in vinegar is acetic acid, which can be used for a variety of acidifying and oxidizing tasks."
6. **Lemon.** "The active cleaning ingredient in lemons is citric acid. Lemons acidify and oxidize, and they smell nice."
7. **Salt.** "Sodium chloride has mild antiseptic and disinfecting qualities. It also has abrasive qualities."
8. **Washing soda.** "Washing soda is hydrated sodium carbonate, an alkali similar to lye but much less powerful. It's available at most grocery stores."[179]

I'm not prepared to offer a list of other safe cleaning products, but I'm of the opinion that most of us can reduce our use even of the safest ones. I'm asking myself, "How clean does this thing need to be to not cause harm? At what point are clothes dirty enough to need washing? How much soap is really needed to get something clean? Will vinegar or baking soda work as well as detergent or scrubbing powder, and how little of even those will do the job?" I'd like to move away from petroleum-based detergents, and as things wind down, our favorite commercial products may cease to be available.

In the past, the soapwort plant was commonly grown and used as soap. I haven't raised the plant or made soap from it, but soapwort is said to be easy to grow and I found soap-making instructions. "The saponin properties found in soapwort plant are responsible for creating the bubbles that produce soap. You can easily make your own liquid soap simply by taking about twelve leafy stems and adding them to a pint of water. This is usually boiled for about 30 minutes and then cooled and strained. Alternatively, you can start out with this small, easy recipe using only a cup of crushed, loosely packed soapwort leaves and 3 cups of boiling water. Simmer for about 15 to 20 minutes on low heat. Allow to cool and then strain. The soap only keeps for a short period (about a week) so use it right away."[180]

The standard homesteading way to make soap is with hardwood ashes, rainwater, and fat. Instructions can be found in many sources, perhaps the most famous being *The Foxfire Books*,[181] the collection of Appalachian folk mores that includes most of the skills people needed as they settled that part of the United States. Both new and used copies are available, and a PDF of Volume One can be read online.[182]

For scrubbing, there is the horsetail plant, genus *Equisetum*, also called Common scouring rush (*E. hyemale*). It has been used historically for scouring pots and pans or for polishing wood and tools, due to its abrasive stems. Simply crush and dry it and use like sandpaper. Wear gloves when harvesting and working with the plant.[183] Take thought before planting it. Horsetail is invasive and persistent. Grow it only in a container, one without drainage holes.

It is certain that the exquisite attention to cleanliness that has become standard in modern life won't survive long in a post-industrial setting. Rather than a shift toward carelessness, however, I hope the focus will move toward an emphasis on health considerations. Scientists are telling us to expect an increase in insect-borne disease and animal-to-human viruses, and with higher night temperatures, human bodies will not have the restoration time they need for recovery. With such increased perils to consider, I think we'll be wise to invest our energies toward real protection, not concerns about appearance. Dirt is not what is dangerous.

Other resources

Carla Emery, *The Encyclopedia of Country Living* (Seattle: Sasquatch Books, 2012). The book that is being sold as the 50th anniversary edition is really a collection of the editions Carla has written since 1969. As a rural housewife learning to master the intricacies of living on the land, she gathered information from the oldsters within her reach as well as from her many acquaintances throughout the country. She aspired to include all the knowledge a person might need to live well without the props of city life. This is fun to read as well as informative.

Two very complete online soapmaking guides are "Grandpappy's Homemade Soap Recipe"[184] and "How to Make Soap from Homemade Lye (including How to Make Lye from Ashes.)"[185] Both of these sites also include information about other useful pre-or-post-industrial skills.

David the Good, *Compost Everything: The Good Guide to Extreme Composting* (FL: Good Books Publishing, 2021).

Joseph C. Jenkins, *The Humanure Handbook*, Fourth edition (Grove City PA: Joseph Jenkins, 2019).

CONCLUSION
A TIME FOR THE FUTURE-ORIENTED

We are in the place of getting wet,
the white knuckle moment,
holding on
not knowing where the lightning strikes next.
It's here.
Collapse, that looming truth,
Erosion, endings, and nothing to be done.
An insatiable rumbling
that will have its way -
And we, the unwitting people of prophecy,
Summoned to unteachable courage.

KRISTOPHER DRUMMOND[186]

All through these handbooks I've kept the spotlight on how we can manage the problems that will surely accompany the end of an age. We've been looking at how to deal with the difficulties, not on the difficulties themselves. A person who reads a handbook on collapse can be counted on to know some of the shape of things to come, of course, and I have mentioned a few consequences we can expect to see as industrial civilization nears its end.

In these last words, though, I want to say something about the peril we are in. The Post Carbon Institute uses the terms destabilization, breakdown, and collapse as parts of a continuum, the far end of which is collapse. By all signs we are now in the stage of destabilization: the biggest stores still offer the most common products at prices somewhat affordable; the power grid is still generally reliable except on the hottest days; and government agencies still render some services with reasonable promptness.

But I think most of us will live to see the period of breakdown. For ordinary people, that means everything becomes less dependable. When something breaks, it will be hard-to-impossible to replace it. We'll have rolling blackouts, boiling water advisories, and bridges out not just for months but for years. What we won't have are insurance companies, hospitals except in the large cities, and new construction. Areas of the

US industrial Rust Belt and rural South have been like that for decades.

How much unrest is likely to occur among those who have already been dealt all the hardship they can manage? People stuck in situations almost inhuman, lacking wholesome spiritual and social support, may only become more desperate. And of course there are individuals, themselves safe enough materially, who would see the distress as their chance to gain power. Social strife and lawlessness will be part of the picture.

It would not be wasted effort to plan how we would meet each of these developments. It seems to me, however, that the most important asset a person can have when confronted with trouble is composure, and a deeper composure is the asset I've hoped to offer readers in these handbooks. But can my instruction move us with poise through descending conditions?

Because I was advising readers to develop spiritual muscle, assemble firm social ties, and learn new skills at this stage of relative stability, my tone may not have conveyed the full strengths of these approaches. I would like to look at the ground again to make sure it can hold us as conditions become more dire.

Reviewing the three handbooks

1. FIND FOOTING THAT DOES NOT DISAPPEAR, THOUGH IT IS UNSEEN

In Handbook One I related how, for me, the most visible form of spirit is found in the eternal verities such as love, truth and fairness. By "seeing" and aligning myself with these forms of goodness—by loving them—I am in touch with a reality beyond the often frightening, sometimes dangerous events of the tangible world. I realize people born into the third century of Western rationalism have trouble sensing security by any means other than the physical: arms, possessions, distance from harm or nearness to a visible version of protection.

If we want to know safety when it no longer exists in the material sense, though, we must find it in the inner realm. I found this safety when I was very young, when there was no help for me anywhere else. I think a seeker of any age will find it by assuming the same circumstance: inadequacy, helplessness, and longing. In other words, to recognize this support, a person may have to feel the need for it.

When we seek, we will find. My consciousness is part of the consciousness of the whole stream of being, which is aware of me whether I attend to it or not. I feel comfortable saying that it loves me. As it is made of love, it loves everything without reservation. A spiritual practice gives opportunity to experience this unqualified, ever-present realm of security. We don't have to believe in it, we only have to accept its gifts.

2. MOVE TOWARD EACH OTHER GUIDED BY EVOLUTIONARY WISDOM

In Handbook Two I identified the lack of connection as being at the root of the crisis we are in. People of our era don't tend to recognize our bonds with each other and with the whole stream of life, and that is not only the ultimate cause of the crisis, but also an impediment to managing it.

Our bondedness exists whether it is recognized or not, however, and the actions we take can help to bring it into view. Although the temptation may be to withdraw behind closed doors when institutional order begins to erode, the response consistent with our evolution is to venture toward others. At these times neighbors need to see each other's faces, share stories and fears, and give mutual reassurance. An immediate problem requiring co-operation to resolve can bring people together. But they may need someone to take the lead, someone who has studied human nature, learned social protocols, and reaches toward others with an open heart.

> *The leadership skills that worked well in the past no longer are sufficient. Warriors for the Human Spirit have only two "weapons" — compassion and insight. They learn how to calm situations of conflict and distress by offering their presence and equanimity. They learn to see what's needed rather than imposing their own needs on a situation. They learn to see beyond their filters and judgments so that more information is available for decision-making.*[187]

These statements, drawn from Margaret Wheatley's "Warriors for the Human Spirit" training program, describe the qualities I believe we will need if we are to be faithful to our obligations as members of the Earth family. When conflict threatens, an openness of this magnitude can only come from the deep springs of spirit. At that time we will move toward each other nudged by inner promptings and on the strength of borrowed courage.

3. USE DISRUPTION TO CREATE A MORE WHOLESOME WAY OF LIFE

In Handbook Three I addressed vital needs that could become the "immediate problem requiring co-operation" that can bring people together. If food runs short, or water, or if conventional sanitation systems fail, the person equipped with the needed skills will be called on by compassion to share them.

I see these accomplishments as more than emergency strategies, however. Instead of being stopgap measures to get us through until we can once again have an underclass to do manual labor, they might become practices of a more equitable and less precarious way of life. Using this kind of knowledge, we might democratize work, investing even menial tasks with worth and creativity. Economic contraction might stimulate personal expansion.

But during a period of disorder would we be left in peace to maintain gardens, purify water, and compost our excrement? A disastrous weather event could destroy much of my work in a few hours. Would I be better off, though, if I had no garden, no alternate water source, and no sustainable means of sanitation? Before and after an interruption, I will still need these essentials, and my knowledge will help to provide them.

We look toward a future we may not live to see

And if I'm not here to benefit, someone else may be. This year the orchard team in my community planted three pecan trees. It will be forty years before they begin bearing well, and no one on the team is under sixty years of age. The trees, to which we must hand-carry water every week for the first three years to make sure they survive, are an investment toward a future that will belong to other generations. We look toward a future we may not live to see.

> *We are prophets of a future not our own.*
> BISHOP KEN UNTENER[188]

My hope for the future, moreover, is not limited to an expectation of human survival here in this place. While we chose trees that would adapt to or even prefer a warmer climate, it seems reasonable to believe that the southeastern region of the United States will be so different in a thousand years that neither trees nor people will be living here. At 450 feet elevation, it may be underwater. Or it may become desert. The future I look to is not tied to what is now familiar.

Although I love the richness of the Cenozoic Era and am doing my best to preserve it, my deeper allegiance is to something bigger and older: the evolutionary stream of the wide, wild cosmos. I came from Earth, and Earth came from the stars, and the stars came from . . . who knows where?

> My Ancestry DNA results came in.
> Just as I suspected, my great-great-grandfather
> was a monarch butterfly.
> Much of who I am is still wriggling under a stone.
> I am part larva, but part hummingbird too.
> There is dinosaur tar in my bone marrow.
> My golden hair sprang out of a meadow in Palestine.
> 3.7 million years ago I swirled in golden dust,
> dreaming of a planet overgrown with lingams and yonis.
> Admit it, you have wings, vast and golden,
> like mine, like mine.
> You have sweat, black and salty,
> like mine, like mine.
> You have secrets silently singing in your blood,
> like mine, like mine.
>
> FRED LAMOTTE[189]

Our lineage goes far back and will go far forward. We live in an unfinished universe. Did we think our version of human would be its final achievement? Evolutionary time is eons beyond measurement, and we are one step toward a future beyond our ability to foresee.

We have yet to move fully into the potential of our humanity

Yet we are here, and we have time to discover the potential of *Homo sapiens*. If we can break out of the cultural mold in which we've been cast, we can live these epic years of planet Earth more as nature intends. Each of us has to determine for ourselves what that means, but I will guess that for most of us, indoctrinated from birth into an individualistic worldview, it will surely call for a more relational experience.

One way this might look is described by author J. Allen Boone:

> People of certain ancient times appear to have been great
> virtuosos in the art of living, particularly skilled in the delicate

science of being in right relations with everything, including animals. . . . Life to these ancients was an all-inclusive kinship in which nothing was meaningless, nothing unimportant, and from which nothing could be excluded. They refused to make any separating barriers between mineral and vegetable, between vegetable and man, or between man and the great primal cause which animates and governs all things.[190]

Boone doesn't document who these people might have been, but his vision fits an ideal that has been forming in my mind for a long time. I wish I had learned as a child to hear the voices of plants. I wish all the lonely Americans—said to be half the population—knew they were not really alone. While we have opportunity, we can begin to repair, for ourselves and the living beings near us, the alienation characteristic of our culture.

Nature also must be asking us for a slower pace, despite the long list of things to do. I like Stephen Covey's four categories of importance:

- Urgent and important
- Not urgent but important
- Urgent but not important
- Not urgent and not important[191]

Only if we withdraw from unnecessary though pressing activity will industrial-era humans discover the joys we may be missing.

In an emergency we focus on what is possible

Most of the people I know are not familiar with the postures and practices that I believe will help us in the coming years. As I've moved deeper into an uncommon perspective, my path has diverged from the typical to the point that I can't talk about myself with much candor except with old friends. The more I become a member of the Earth family in my heart, the harder it becomes to speak of it in conversation. There is no casual cultural shorthand for my current understandings and experiences.

This way of seeing gives me peace, though, and thus will also help these neighbors who, comfortable up to now and barely aware of the true dangers we face, will need my calm as the consequences mount. They may never share my thoughts, but they will share the impacts, and

I am counting on their goodwill to join hands with me to do whatever is necessary and possible.

As circumstances deteriorate, there will be a leveling and a simplification. Likely we will act more than we talk. Going forward we may have to survive with less than we thought we had to have, and we may find we don't have to have it. And when unanticipated troubles arrive to make everything harder than we can predict, and yet somehow we must manage the essential tasks of producing food, obtaining clean water, and providing sanitation, we will need strong spirits and deep relationships to sustain us. We will need all the inner assets humans have developed through millennia of evolution.

What Samwise did as he faced dire prospects in Lord of the Rings is what I expect us to do as we meet each new reality.

> But even as hope died in Sam, or seemed to die, it was turned to a new strength. Sam's plain hobbit face grew stern, almost grim, as the will hardened in him, and he felt through all his limbs a thrill, as if he was turning into some creature of stone and steel that neither despair nor weariness nor endless barren miles could subdue. With a new sense of responsibility he brought his eyes back to the ground near at hand, studying the next move.
>
> TOLKIEN[192]

Like Samwise, we will bring our eyes back to the ground at hand, study the possibilities, and choose the best option available. We may have an interval in which to acquire knowledge about how to live without the machines, materials, and services of our present circumstances. If we are wise, we will spend part of that time seeking out information about how nature manages to accomplish so much, squandering nothing. Only by aligning ourselves with this biological fact will we be able to move toward a stable future for ourselves and other living creatures.

Familiar ways of thinking will not take us safely into the far future

I hope readers now realize why these three handbooks belong together: I am trying to repair a breach. As I have stressed throughout, reality is one great whole: no outside or inside, no line between spiritual, social, and everyday, practical labor. Whereas the worldview we inherited took reality apart in order to tinker with the pieces, going forward we must learn to restore its unity. As mythologist and storyteller Michael Meade said recently, "We are in a collective rite of passage that requires a wide scale awakening to the interconnectedness of all of life."[193]

If we were given back the planet in its pre-industrial glory, would we do something better with it this time? Not if we still lived by the bits-and-pieces basis of our current story. If our view of the world doesn't change, we would repeat the mistakes and end up again with ruin, as now. Let's not do that. Let us take up the challenge of the poet Kristopher Drummond:[194]

> *Step outside this clinging dying normalcy*
> *and dance a jagged lightning jig.*
> *Be the fire burning down this poison forest,*
> *and let the seeds of renewal spill from your mouth.*
> *Set your pen to page and turn your ear to earth.*
> *A new story wants to give you an apple.*

Appendix I
IMPORTANT BOOKS IN MY READING PATH

As I relate in Handbook One, the most pressing issue I was trying to resolve as I entered adulthood was the dissonance between the dominant worldview and my own perception of reality. I had lived in a pocket of US Bible belt culture, without mentors other than writers I encountered in English literature classes, and the seminary-educated ministers who happened to speak at churches I attended. Since I didn't have exact words for my questions and had only books with which to converse on these matters, I read widely and with eager hope. A few books of the more famous thinkers of the twentieth century came my direction, and while I was enriched by them in other ways, I reached midlife without finding authors who addressed my particular concern, which might be phrased, "What is sacred and what is not?" My intuitive position, then tentative but later held with confidence, is "of course everything is sacred!" Or perhaps more precisely: "Sacredness is an aspect of everything."

One of the first books I found that deliberately challenged the dualism that has dominated Western science and religion in the last three centuries was cultural historian Morris Berman's 1989 classic *Coming to Our Senses*. In words I could understand, his book pointed to a fault in Western culture: the split between body and spirit. As I report in the first handbook, although he was far ahead of me in analyzing the problem, I recognized that he wrote about my issue.

Nearby in the library I came across *A New Science of Life* (1981) by biologist Rupert Sheldrake. Sheldrake is not bound by inherited scientific assumptions about reality, but instead works from observation—the posture of any science when true to its mission. He includes ordinary puzzles of life in his research, such as how a pet can know when his master is coming home. In this book he presents the idea of morphic resonance, the theory that bodies extend into fields—morphic fields—that allow creatures to perceive and influence the fields of other beings. He views memory as a basic property of nature, and assumes patterns are contagious: once something happens somewhere, it induces the same thing to happen in other places.[195]

Whether due to morphic resonance or simply because dualism leaves too many phenomena unexplained, it is fairly easy now for a person to come across scientists who are capably refuting the materialist or reductionist orientation. Their work might be labeled the science of the twentieth century, since it began in the century's first years with the quantum mechanics physicists—except for the fact that the arguments they raise are views that have been accepted elsewhere for many centuries. Eastern philosophy and Indigenous societies have almost always seen the connectedness of all things, Earth as a living organism, and nature as sentient.

Wholeness and the Implicate Order (1980) by theoretical physicist David Bohm (mentioned in Handbook One) is one of the early expressions of this understanding. A splendid human being and brilliant scientist, Bohm recognized in quantum physics a clear demonstration that spiritual and physical are not separate categories. What he calls an "implicate" order exists within the more visible world that he calls "explicate."

Eventually my path led me to Western writers who learned to experience the world as Indigenous people tend to do. *Original Wisdom* by Robert Wolff (2001) is an example of first-hand findings that didn't take place in a laboratory. It tells what he encountered living among the aboriginal Sng'oi of Malaysia. A work assignment first sent him to these pre-industrial, pre-agricultural people, but he made a strong connection with them at least partly because he had grown up in Sumatra and was easily able to learn their language. Their shaman took him into the jungle. "We walk," was his teaching. "Don't talk," by which Wolff understood he also meant, "Don't think."

After several walks Wolff considered uneventful, one day he found his senses suddenly awakened. He was thirsty. The shaman knew; he said, "Drink?" but he remained detached. Wolff wrote: "As soon as I stopped thinking, planning, deciding, analyzing—using my mind, in short, I felt as if I was pushed a certain direction. I walked a few steps and immediately saw a big leaf with about a half cup of water in it." As he stared in awe, he perceived a fuller picture. With his whole being he felt and saw the leaf belonging to the tree, belonging to the soil, belonging to the jungle, belonging to the living skin of the Earth. "And nothing was separate; all was one, the same thing: water—leaf—plant—trees—soil—animals—earth—air—sunlight and little wisps of wind, the all-ness was everywhere and I was part of it."[196]

The Spell of the Sensuous by David Abram (1997) tells of being in Indonesia and Nepal where he wandered for several years as an itinerant magician. As he came to villages in remote areas, his magic tricks formed a link with local sorcerers whose welcome brought invitations to enter homes and participate in rituals and ceremonies. While living several years in that atmosphere, Abram came to share the identification with nature that was innate to these cultures, but he lost the ability as he re-entered his US lifestyle. He began to seek out the causes and a cure for Western blindness.

He says the ordinary Western view is that whatever lies beyond laboratory analysis must be "of some other, nonphysical realm above nature, 'supernatural.'" He discovered the work of Merleau-Ponty, who conceived of an "elemental power that has had no name in the entire history of Western philosophy" and which he called "The Flesh"—melding both our flesh and "the flesh of the world." Due to this theory and to his time among Indigenous people, Abram writes, "I find myself forced to acknowledge that any visible, tangible form that meets my gaze may also be an experiencing subject, sensitive and responsive to the beings around it, and to me."[197]

In the 2002 book *Lost Language of Plants* Stephen Harrod Buhner describes the language of the plant world that is found in the chemicals they release to communicate with insects, animals, and other plants—all for the purpose of helping to maintain the stability of the planet. He writes,

> Imagine a ball of twine the exact size and shape of Earth. Better yet, telephone line. Take the end point of line and weave it back into the beginning so there is no beginning and no end. Every place the line crosses itself (you could think of them as synaptic junctions) messages cross over; communication travels quickly throughout the line itself as well. . . . Each plant, plant neighborhood, plant community, ecosystem and biome has messages flowing through it constantly—trillions and trillions of messages at the same time. . . . Impacts at one point affect every other point in the system.[198]

One day as I read his words about this interconnected web between plants and their surroundings, his words spoke to me in a new way of my own nestedness within the immense Earth organism. Suddenly I felt greatly cared for and potentially more useful as I saw myself within the interlinked whole, an assurance I captured in an affirmation I created based on his text:

> *My life is so closely coupled with the physical and chemical environment of which it is a part that it cannot legitimately be viewed in isolation from it. The physical and chemical environment is a world-wide interconnected biofeedback loop that monitors conditions with the goal of maintaining Earth's homeostasis. May my words, thoughts, and actions likewise contribute.*

Thomas Berry's 1988 book *The Dream of the Earth* came into my hands at a neighbor's yard sale.[199] I hadn't heard of that particular Berry, and it went unread on my bookshelf for more than a year. When I did start reading it around the year 2000, my mouth dropped open. Here was a Passionist priest expressing these same views about the unity of life. Shortly after, when I had the opportunity to meet Thomas (as his followers in the Berry community call him), I showed him that my copy had been so thoroughly highlighted as to make most of the pages pink, which was the highlighter color I used at the time. A famous Berry quotation is "The universe is a communion of subjects, not a collection of objects."[200]

When I had more leisure time I began to read fiction again. Looking back at the books that have given me the most enjoyment, I see that each has fed my spirit by illuminating one or more of the eternal verities.

The Secret Garden by Frances Hodgson Burnett (1911)[201] has been one of my bedtime stories for several years—as a mature adult; I didn't discover it in childhood. I recorded most of the text on one of the small voice recorders that I listen to routinely as I go to sleep at night. The transformation of two untaught, emotionally abandoned and therefore generally disagreeable children, through their encounter with a likewise neglected piece of ground that had once been a garden, reaches mythical proportions that rise above the author's period language and cultural biases. Along with nature, a few servants of the household come forward to offer at last the kind of guidance and attention the children have lacked.

An act reflecting generosity is central to the redemption of the orphaned Mary Lennox, who was sent to live at Misselthwaite Manor.

Mrs. Sowerby, mother of Mary's personal maid Martha, takes crucial pennies of her family's meager income to buy Mary a skipping rope. The gift builds the child's health by taking her out of doors, which leads to the discovery of the garden, which in turn redeems Mary, who then is agent of redemption for the invalid heir. With the help of Martha's brother Dickon and the gardener, eventually as they tend the garden's beauty, the children bring change into the life of the boy's immature father.

The theme of transformation is also clearly seen in the much-loved Jane Austen novel, *Pride and Prejudice* (1813).[202] The heroine and hero separately engage in courageous self-examination and alteration before they can come toward each other as wiser and more humble people. I think humility is the primary virtue they exhibit, but as in all of this author's books, courtesy is also a prominent principle. Austin pays minute attention to the speech and actions of her characters and to the effect these have on other people. She upholds standards of social sophistication and interpersonal respect that are almost unknown in our bolder, more thoughtless day. To me these manners provide a welcome insight into how we ourselves might behave if our lives were not so fast and noisy, if we took more time for caution and subtlety.

Lord of the Rings by JRR Tolkien (1954), LOTR to millions of readers, is another book from which I've made recordings for sleep-time relaxation. The words of the scenes I like best go through my mind in idle moments all through the day. Since I first read it, the exquisite language, rugged outdoor setting, and honorable characters have become part of my life. That is the gift of fiction: to bring other lives in other places and eras into our more limited experience.

In summary, the reading trail I followed supported my desire to follow the verities, in particular the principle of truth. These books supplied information that had been lacking in my education, and they encouraged me to live by my own best intuition. My gratitude to their authors is beyond words.

Appendix II
FORMING A MINI-VILLAGE

I hope I can join with a group of people who use their differences to work as equals toward mutually chosen goals that will take time and effort to achieve.

As circumstances grow more difficult and customary public services fail, we will be fortunate if we can join with nearby others to furnish daily necessities. A neighborhood group with an assortment of skills and knowledge may enable people to stay in their homes. It may help them maintain health—mental and physical. In every neighborhood there are likely to be a few people with similar needs who are willing to pool resources and look together for ways to deal with worsening circumstances. Handbook Two is intended to help us prepare to become valuable members of such informal alignments, but we must then apply our skills to gather our neighbors into a helpful alliance.

> How will we organize with the people around us to provide whatever markets or public institutions may fail to deliver?
>
> How do we create alliances that have the potential to hang together through hard times?

Now is the time to get to know your neighbors

If you are reading these handbooks while living conditions are generally stable, this is the ideal time to begin planning for closer neighborhood cohesion. The kind of preparation you can make now will serve both for emergencies and for daily living.

> *Social scientists studying modern human responses to natural disasters or to sudden collective deprivation have noted a typical pattern of behavior: initially, people pull together. They share what they have, volunteering their efforts to help neighbors and strangers. However, if scarcity continues for many months or years, then cooperative behavior gradually dwindles, and each individual's circle of trust diminishes significantly.*[203]

Emergencies do tend to draw people together—at least at first, but it will take skill, careful planning, and a large store of goodwill to help neighbors continue the altruistic behavior in the following months. Our culture has taught us to see ourselves as separate individuals, separate from each other and from the rest of nature. Even though it is rarely to our advantage to live that way, it is a hard habit to break. It helps to acknowledge that the goal we want to accomplish is not normal behavior in most places. We must give our neighbors time to get used to a new pattern of thinking.

In many ways the intentional community where I live now looks like a normal suburban development of small homes, except that it is in a rural area on the edge of a tiny town. We are organized under state law as a homeowners association, and individual properties are bought and sold according to legal regulations. But buyers also sign a covenant with the community that declares our intention to live together sharing values such as environmental sustainability.

Most people who buy these lots or homes know they are joining a community, and that is their intention, hence the term "intentional." Still, we all come from the individualistic culture, and if we are to live more communally, we must learn how by trial and error, just as people in more typical neighborhoods must. Moreover, many of us have formed ties with people in the town. When I think of banding together in time of trouble, I'm also thinking of the people I know at the town office, the fire station, the library, the restaurant, and the church. What I would do here to gather a supportive group for meeting problems and emergencies is much the same as I would do in other places.

Based on my experiences in both intentional and unintentional neighborhoods, I will offer one possible scenario that shows how a cluster of households might become a mini-village. Since transportation may become an issue at some point, I'm envisioning a group of people with easy access to each other.

Parties and shared meals are a good way to begin getting acquainted

Two or three friends might begin by hosting neighborhood gatherings that are almost purely social but have the serious purpose of getting to know each other better. Block or cul-de-sac parties are a standard American custom and can seem an ordinary thing to do. The get-togethers may include local amateur musicians and unchallenging games, outdoors if weather is favorable.

As people talk, they may reveal their qualifications to become long-term-survival team members. Strategic questions may draw out helpful information about their lives that might answer questions such as these:

> Have they demonstrated social tendencies? If they seem to get along with others at this social event, conversation may reveal a history of valuing their membership in other groups (churches, lodges, PTA's).
>
> Do they show a good bit of energy? Some very nice people simply don't have enough physical stamina to accept more responsibility. They may need the help of the worker team, but they won't be regular contributors.
>
> Will they be dependable? If they've held responsible positions in employment or volunteer work, their accounts of these experiences may give clues about reliability.
>
> Do their stories tend to be about positive outcomes? Sometimes people exchange problem stories with bad outcomes because the general talk gets going that direction. To test that possibility, the hosts can try to turn the conversation toward positive experiences, perhaps in former times or at younger ages.

It is good to keep track of the abilities and assets revealed in these informal gatherings: who has experience doing home repair, plumbing, gardening, sewing? Who keeps unusual tools? Does the neighborhood have a doctor, nurse, mechanic, carpenter, plumber, minister or priest, attorney?

Conversation will reveal current concerns

Conversation at these gatherings inevitably covers concerns caused by a change in conditions. If you live in a drought-prone region, for example, people may talk about water issues. And if they don't, and you anticipate the day when water will become a problem, you may introduce the topic in a non-alarming way. The question "How do you think we can forestall water rationing?" casts no blame, even asked of a neighbor who maintains a large grass lawn. If a neighborhood conversation on water conservation is to develop, in fact, by all means it should include those least aware of the impact of their usage. An "us" and "them" dynamic is always counterproductive.

As conditions worsen, you can expect there will be more shared concerns. In conversation you may identify people whose concerns match yours or whose knowledge or skill matches your need.

Food prices are likely to continue rising as fires, floods, and high temperatures interfere with food production.

Power grids may become unreliable, since electric utilities have not been required by state governments to upgrade their plants and grids to meet new climate realities.

Water and sewer systems may break down because cities have not maintained or replaced aging pipes (and many have turned part of these services over to out-of state private companies, which have cost-saving rather than service as a priority).

Storms, fire, and flooding already hamper delivery of services by hospitals, fire departments, and police stations, and few of these have in their budgets the funds to upgrade facilities.

The profit-based medical system was not designed to keep people well, and even local emergency care may become unavailable in many places.

EARLY INFORMAL GROUPINGS

Work trades and other forms of bartering occur naturally as neighbors become acquainted, and they can be the beginning of larger alliances.

If two or more households identify a shared need, they may quickly agree to address it together. One example might be difficulty in obtaining certain food staples. Someone might offer to make the trip across town, collect money from others, and call everyone when the trip has taken place.

If the idea of a buying club is appealing to several households, more formal arrangements may be needed. Someone could research sources, another could place the order, another could make the trip to the destination, another could keep records of who wanted what item, who paid for what, and collect money. Members might exchange phone numbers and if needed, addresses. This group might form the basis of a more permanent alliance with broader concerns.

Once a pattern of group purchasing is established, it might be used for other items, even large purchases. The group might want to share cost and maintenance of certain assets.

Getting deeper into organization

A good size for a semi-permanent group addressing common problems would be twelve to fifteen individuals (representing no more than twenty households), a number small enough to meet in homes and exchange information between meetings, and not so large that any cash accumulation might be a temptation. When a compatible group seems to have coalesced more or less naturally, they might discuss a more formal alignment. At that point they might consider different patterns of organization.

Let's say they decide to call themselves a support team to meet physical and material needs (rather than emotional ones).

They decide that most of their activities will be kept private, though not secret. They want to be able to store a few supplies and occasionally collect money without its being noticed, and they want to be free to occasionally reveal relevant personal information such as finances in a confidential setting. But it is important to maintain neighborliness with all nearby residents, through larger group activities as well as less formal friendships.

They may outline meeting practices, which might include protocols such as these:

Take turns speaking.

Give everybody a chance to talk.

Make decisions on a consensus basis. Often a proposal under consideration will be either the obvious choice, or one that has been discussed informally outside the meeting structure. When consensus can't be reached, they may decide to move forward on a proposal if only one person objects.

Encourage careful listening.

Speak in "I" statements.

Maintain confidentiality.

Keep meetings short and infrequent.

They may want to choose a facilitator for each meeting. In addition, they may find that accurate notes of previous meetings would have been helpful. They begin keeping minutes. Someone might volunteer or the duty could be rotated.

They would also divide responsibility to store goods and currency when purchases are involved, so that valuables are scattered among members. But they might select one person to maintain a permanent record of receipts and disbursements, whether these are money or materials, "electing" the responsible party in order to create a sound audit trail. One person may volunteer to safely archive all other written records, such as minutes.

With these structures in place, the group can concentrate on their mission: to live together as well as possible in deteriorating circumstances. Having fun together will be essential to that goal: the more music and dancing, games and sports, and shared meals and treats, the better. And social events can be a way to include the larger community.

Resolving contentious issues

Eventually issues may arise on which the core group is deeply divided. Rather than giving up on the idea of working together, a nine-step consensus process might operate as follows:

1. If a matter isn't easily agreed on, there will be discussion. Each viewpoint is voiced, expressed as specific concerns or alternatives. The recommendation may be refined at this point.
2. After discussion, another vote will be taken at the same meeting—either on the original or a refined recommendation.
3. If it does not pass by consensus the second time, it goes to a smaller group, a committee chosen by the entire alliance, composed of no more than three members.
4. When the sub-group meets, those blocking or anyone interested in the issue will come to the meeting to discuss their concerns.
5. After listening to the concerns and discussing more, the sub-group will make a recommendation at the next group meeting. This could include a majority/minority recommendation.
6. At the next group meeting, the recommendation will be discussed again and perhaps refined.
7. After discussion, the original or refined recommendation will come up for consensus a third time. The agenda for this meeting will have been announced and will have included the possibility of a vote.
8. If the group is still not able to come to consensus, and there is a quorum present, a vote will be taken. (The group has to determine the number that constitutes a quorum.) A two-thirds majority vote of those present is required to adopt the recommendation.
9. Once a decision is reached, action steps and timelines will be created.

Organizing to address specific needs and problems

TRANSPORTATION

Private transportation may become less practical. Two households might agree to maintain one vehicle together. Or a member for whom independent transportation is a priority might offer to provide occasional taxi service. Members might agree that having at least one vehicle available to the neighborhood for emergencies is important enough to subsidize.

GARDENING

Those interested in growing food together may form a separate team. Each might set aside a portion of their property for this purpose, so that each grows a different set of food crops. They could pool effort and money for shared tools and supplies, including soil amendments. One lot that seems suitable might be chosen for a neighborhood compost bin, with the work of maintenance shared by all. The gardening instructions in Handbook Three can provide a foundation primer.

PRESERVING FOODS AND BEVERAGES

Some members may have experience and equipment for home food preservation (canning and lactic acid fermentation) or home brewing.

SANITATION

At an advanced stage of co-operation and trust, some households might begin composting humanure, using Joseph Jenkins' method as outlined in Handbook Three.

EMOTIONAL SUPPORT

Although all have agreed to keep general meetings short and as infrequent as possible, after several weeks they may realize that pressing individual problems are having an impact on the group's work. They might add an opportunity for expressions of grief or anxiety—either at the regular meetings or at a separate time.

For example, they might add an item to the agenda: a check in. At the beginning of the time together, each person might be given a two-minute opportunity to share information about individual situations. Members would not respond to these statements verbally during the meeting, but they would have that information to act on later.

Or they might organize a buddy system for members interested in this kind of sharing.

SAFETY AND SECURITY

As society moves into breakdown, safety becomes everyone's responsibility. The first rule of safety is to avoid dangerous situations.

One reason to band together is for protection against assault, vandalism, and theft. It is important to identify sites and activities that would pose the most risk. People could agree not to go out alone at night or not to drive significant distances alone. A buddy system might fill that need.

If hospitals are far away, it becomes even more important to avoid injury: no going up on roofs or handling dangerous equipment without backup, for example.

Heatstroke will become more common. At 95°F with high humidity the body doesn't perspire to cool off.

Roaming animals may increasingly be a problem.

Vigilance includes close observance of questionable behavior in neighbors.

It is important to recognize that a neighbor might become a source of danger: someone who shows extreme antisocial manner, for example, whether abnormally quiet and withdrawn, or disruptive.

There may be children who exhibit signs of abuse: unusual fearfulness, bullying, injuring animals or other children.

Indications of spousal abuse: secretiveness, submissiveness, and trying to be perfect in the victim; aggressiveness, uncontrolled anger, secretiveness in the victimizer.

Signs of mental instability, including a suicide attempt.

A few people in every population, usually males, could be classified as clinically antisocial. While there are differences of opinion among psychologists regarding these deviations from the normal, it is clear that there is no place for them in an alliance of neighbors committed to helping each other during hard times. If supportive law enforcement is unavailable to remove disruptive individuals, ingenuity must serve.

Farther down the road they may seek special training

First aid

Herbal medicine

Self-defense

De-escalation techniques

Non-violent communication (NVC)

Disaster response

Beer brewing

Low-energy food preservation: lactic acid fermentation, canning, drying

CONCLUDING WORDS

I've read that the two greatest worries people have are the fear of being overwhelmed by the conditions of the world and the fear of feeling abandoned and left all alone. A mini-village answers both worries.

Co-operating (operating together as equal partners) is nevertheless a new thing. I commend your interest in forming this kind of venture. It could be lifesaving, but it will not be easy. When I am trying to be part of a team making difficult decisions, I sometimes remind myself of these affirmations:

I can rely on the humanity of my neighbors, even those who seem unlike me.

Humans, while each is unique, do not step outside their combined heredity and enculturation.

I know the outer limits of their needs and motivations, for we are of the same species.

All acts are an attempt to meet needs.

Communication skills strengthen our ability to remain human, even under trying conditions.

May the force of our long history as social beings be with you!

Appendix III

CAWST BIOSAND FILTER CONSTRUCTION MANUAL: CONSTRUCTION STAGES B, E, AND H

The entire manual can be found at
https://sswm.info/sites/default/files/reference_attachments/CAWST%20 2009%20Biosand%20Filter%20Manual.pdf
12, 2916 – 5th Avenue, Calgary, Alberta, T2A 6K4, Canada
phone: + 1 403.243.3285 | fax : + 1 403.243.6199
email: cawst@cawst.org | website: www.cawst.org

CAWST is a Canadian non-profit organization focused on the principle that clean water changes lives. Safe water and basic sanitation are fundamentals necessary to empower the world's poorest people and break the cycle of poverty. CAWST believes that the place to start is to teach people the skills they need to have safe water in their homes. CAWST transfers knowledge and skills to organizations and individuals in developing countries through education, training and consulting services. This ever expanding network can motivate individual households to take action to meet their own water and sanitation needs. One of CAWST's core strategies is to make knowledge about water common knowledge. This is achieved, in part, by developing and freely distributing education materials with the intent of increasing its availability to those who need it most.

This document is open content and licensed under the Creative Commons Attribution Works 3.0 Unported License. To view a copy of this license, visit http://creativecommons.org/licenses/by/3.0/ or send a letter to Creative Commons, 171 Second Street, Suite 300, San Francisco, California 94105, USA.

You are free to: Share—to copy, distribute and transmit this document.

STAGE B – LOCATE THE SAND AND GRAVEL (PAGE 17)

Selecting and preparing the filtration sand and gravel is crucial for the treatment efficiency of the biosand filter. While not complicated, the steps in preparing the filtration sand must be followed exactly as presented. Poor selection and preparation of the filtration sand could lead to poor performance and a considerable amount of work to rectify the problem.

Recommended Source

Obtaining and preparing the sand: Crushed rock is the best type of filtration sand since it has less chance of being contaminated with pathogens or organic material. This sand also has less uniform sizing of the grains. A mixture of grain sizes is required for the proper functioning of the filter. Gravel pits or quarries are the best place to obtain crushed rock, and are common in most parts of the world. You can also ask local construction, road work, or brick manufacturing companies to find out where they get their source of crushed rock. At first, quarry rock may not seem proper for sieving due to the large amounts of dust. You can select the rock load and the crusher properly to ensure that large chunks of rock and dust are minimal. Often, you can even sieve the load at the quarry site and only pay for what you take. This greatly reduces waste and the cost. Crushed rock may be difficult to locate, more expensive, and require transportation to your production site. However, it is critical in providing the best water quality and is worth the extra time, effort and cost. If crushed rock is absolutely not available, the next choice is sand from high on the banks of a river (that has not been in the water), followed by sand found in the riverbed itself. The last choice is beach sand.

Table 2

Properties to Look for when Selecting the Filtration Sand

Should	Should NOT
• When you pick up a handful of the sand, you should be able to feel the coarseness of the grains.	• It should not contain any organic material (e.g. leaves, grass, sticks, loam, dirt).
• You should be able to clearly see the individual grains, and the grains should be of different sizes and shapes.	• It should not contain possible microbiological contamination. Avoid areas that have been used frequently by people or animals.
• When you squeeze a handful of dry sand, and then you open your hand, the sand should all pour smoothly out of your hand.	• It should not be very fine sand or sand that is mostly silt and clay.
• Sand with a lot of gravel, up to 12 mm (½") in diameter, should be used. Using gravel larger than 12 mm (½") is waste and will not be used in filter construction or as drainage gravel.	• When you squeeze a handful of dry sand, it should not ball up in your hand or stick to your hand. If it does, it probably contains a lot of dirt or clay.

The DRY sand must be passed through the 12 mm (½") sieve, the 6 mm (¼") sieve, the 1 mm (0.04") sieve and the 0.7 mm (0.03") in that order.

1. Discard the material that does not pass through the 12 mm (½") sieve.
2. Store the material that is captured by the 6 mm (¼") sieve – this is used for your drainage gravel layer.
3. Store the material that is captured by the 1 mm (0.04") sieve – this is used for your separating gravel layer.
4. Store the material that is captured by the 0.7 mm (0.03") sieve – A portion of this material is used to make the concrete filter box while the other portion is sieved further to make the filtration sand.
5. The material that passes through the 0.7 mm (0.03") sieve is the filtration sand that goes into your filter. If constructing concrete

filters, this sand should NOT be mixed with cement because it is too fine and will not produce good quality concrete.

Wash the gravel:
1. Place about 2–3 litres (0.5–1 gallon) of 12 mm (½") gravel in a container.
2. Put twice as much water in the container.
3. Using your hand, swirl the gravel around until the water becomes quite dirty.
4. Pour the dirty water out of the container.
5. Repeat the process until the water in your container is clear.
6. Wash the rest of the 12 mm (½") gravel, using the same method (a little at a time).
7. Repeat steps 1 to 6 for the 6 mm (¼") gravel.
8. Place all of the gravel on a cover or concrete surface in the sun to dry. This step is especially important if the gravel or the wash water might be microbiologically contaminated.
9. Store the gravel under cover to keep it dry. You can also package it in bags or containers ready for use in the installation process (see Stage G Installation).

Wash the filtration sand:
1. Put a small amount of the 0.7 mm (0.03") sand in the container (approximately 10 cm (4") deep).
2. Put double the amount of water in the container.
3. Using your hand, swirl the sand around the container 10 times very quickly, making sure your fingers touch the bottom of the container and get all of the sand moving.
4. Quickly decant the dirty water.
5. Repeat steps 1 to 4 as many times as determined in the flow rate testing section. Do NOT wash the sand until the water in your container is clean. *This residual water should still be somewhat dirty.* It takes time and practice to be able to know how much to wash the sand.
6. Wash the rest of the sand using the same method (steps 1 to 5).

7. Place all of the sand and gravel on a tarp or concrete surface in the sun to dry. This step is especially important if the sand, gravel, or the wash water might be biologically contaminated.
8. Store the sand under cover once it is dry. You can also package it in bags or containers to make it ready for transport and installation.
9. As you wash, count the number of times that you decant your container.
10. Initially, it is a trial and error process – but that is why it's important to count how many times you wash the sand, so that once you get the correct flow rate, you can repeat the same process. To estimate if the sand has been washed adequately, put some sand into a clear container with an equal amount of clear water. Put the lid on and swirl it. Looking from the side of the container, 3–4 seconds after you stop swirling, you should be able to see the surface of the sand.
11. Your sand and gravel sources may vary so the number of times that you wash the sand will have to be adjusted periodically, but after some time you should develop the ability to know when the sand has been adequately washed, just by looking at the wash water in your container.

Flow rate test

1. For the final test of the sand, install a biosand filter on site using your filtration sand and gravel, and test the flow rate. The flow rate should be 0.4 L/minute when the filter is installed.
2. If the flow rate is much greater than 0.4 L/minute, the sand has been washed too much. You must decrease the number of times that you wash the sand. A flow rate that is too fast is not acceptable – the filter will not be effective.
3. If the flow rate is much less than 0.4 L/minute, the sand hasn't been washed enough. You must increase the number of times that you wash the sand. The filter will still function if the flow rate is too slow, but it may plug more often, requiring more frequent maintenance. If the flow rate is just slightly less than 0.4 L/minute, it can be left as is – as long as the flow rate isn't so slow that it is inconvenient for the user.

STAGE D – CONSTRUCT THE FILTER BOX

PLASTIC OUTLET TUBE (page 25)

PREPARE THE MOLD (page 26)

POUR THE FILTER (page 27)

REMOVE FILTER FROM MOLD (page 30)

STAGE E – CONSTRUCT THE DIFFUSER (PAGE 31)

The purpose of the diffuser is to prevent any disturbance of the sand surface and biolayer when water is added to the top of the filter. It is essential for the correct operation of the filter so that pathogens do not penetrate far into the sand bed. There are several types of diffusers that can be built—each with its own advantages and limitations. The one that you choose to build will depend on your skill level, the tools and materials that are available, and the preference of the user.

DESIGN SPECIFICATIONS:

- 3 mm (1/8") diameter holes in a 2.5 cm x 2.5 cm (1" x 1") grid pattern. Larger holes will result in disturbance of the surface of the sand. Smaller holes will restrict the flow through the filter, possibly causing the flow rate to drop.
- There should not be a gap between the edge of the diffuser and the concrete filter. A gap allows water to travel along the walls of the filter, rather than being distributed evenly through the holes of the diffuser plate.
- A tight fit will also prevent a diffuser made of light material from floating. Tips:
  - Many materials have been used for the diffusers – sheet metal, plastic, and concrete. Galvanized sheet metal is recommended since it is more durable and lasts longer. If poorly galvanized sheet metal is used, it will rust quickly and eventually need to be replaced. Avoid using any material that will rot or cause the growth of mold or algae in the presence of water (e.g. wood).
  - The metal diffuser box design is recommended since it does not let water to travel down the walls of the filter. This type of diffuser is needed for the arsenic version of the filter or to retrofit previous versions of the filter to the Version 10 design. If you choose to construct the metal diffuser box, it is also recommended that you

also construct the lid with galvanized sheet metal. This lid will fit nicely over the entire filter, including the metal flaps of the diffuser box that will hang off the top edge of the filter.

STAGE F – CONSTRUCT THE LID
STAGE G – INSTALLATION
STAGE H – OPERATION, MAINTENANCE AND FOLLOW-UP

ESTABLISHING THE BIOLAYER (page 53)

The biolayer is the key component of the filter that removes pathogens. Without it, the filter removes about 30-70% of the pathogens through mechanical trapping and adsorption. The ideal biolayer will increase the treatment efficiency up to 99% removal of pathogens.

It may take up to 30 days for the biolayer to fully form. During that time, both the removal efficiency and the oxygen demand will increase as the biolayer grows. The biolayer is NOT visible – it is NOT a green slimy coating on top of the sand. The filtration sand may turn a darker colour, but this is due to the suspended solids that have become trapped.

The water from the filter can be used during the first few weeks while the biolayer is being established, but disinfection, as always, is recommended during this time.

DAILY USE (page 53)

All household users, including children, need to be taught how and why the filter works and about its correct operation and maintenance. Children are frequently the main users of the filter. Proper use includes the following practices:

- Use the filter at least once every 1–2 days, preferably 2–4 times each day.
- Use the same source of water every day to improve the treatment efficiency.
- Use the best source of water (least contaminated) that is available — the better the source water, the better the treated water will be.
- The turbidity of the source water should be less than 50 NTU. If it is more turbid, then sediment or strain the water before using the biosand filter.
- The diffuser must always be in place when pouring water into the filter — never pour water directly onto the sand layer. Slowly pour the water into the filter.

- The lid should always be kept on the filter.
- Use a separate container for collecting the source water.
- Use a separate safe storage container that has the following qualities:
    - Strong and tightly fitting lid or cover
    - Tap or narrow opening at the outlet
    - Stable base so it doesn't tip over
    - Durable and strong
    - Should not be transparent (see-through)
    - Easy to clean
- Store treated water off the ground in a shady place in the home.
- Store treated water away from small children and animals.
- Drinking treated water as soon as possible, preferably the same day.
- Water must always be allowed to flow freely from the filter. Do NOT plug the outlet or connect a hose to it. Plugging the outlet tube could increase the water level in the filter, which could kill the biolayer due to lack of oxygen. Putting a hose or other device on the outlet can also siphon or drain the water in the filter, dropping the water level below the sand layer and drying out the filter.
- Do NOT store food inside the filter. Some users want to store their food on the diffuser because it is a cool location. The water in the top of the filter is contaminated, so it will contaminate the food. Also, the food attracts insects to the filter.
- The filtered water should always be disinfected to ensure the highest quality.

> **TIP:** The sound of water dripping from the outlet into the storage container can be irritating. The closer you place the container to the outlet, the less noise there will be. A container with a small opening also reduces dripping noise and prevents recontamination of the filtered water.

MAINTENANCE (page 55)

There are some key maintenance tasks that are required after a filter has been installed and used regularly.

The outlet tube will become contaminated during normal use via dirty hands, animals, or insects. Clean the outlet tube regularly with soap and water or a chlorine solution.

Clean the inside of the treated water storage container when it looks

dirty, when you do regular maintenance or at least once a month. **Do NOT pour chlorine into the top of the filter – it will kill the biolayer.** To clean the storage container:
- Wash your hands before cleaning the container.
- Scrub the inside of the container with soap and treated water.
- Empty the soapy water through the tap.
- Rinse the container with a little treated water.
- Add chlorine to water in the storage container – let it sit for 30 minutes – if chlorine is not available, let the container air dry.
- Empty the remaining water through the tap.
- Clean the tap with a clean cloth and chlorine solution (such as bleach).

The entire filter should be cleaned regularly (e.g. lid, diffuser, outside surfaces).

Chlorine works well to disinfect the treated water and clean surfaces, but do NOT pour chlorine into the top of the filter.

SWIRL & DUMP (page 56)

The flow rate through the filter will slow down over time as the biolayer develops and suspended solids are trapped in the upper layer of the sand. Users will know when the "swirl & dump" is required because the flow rate will drop to an unacceptable level. The filter is still effectively treating the water at this point; however the length of time that it takes to get a container of filtered water may become too long and be inconvenient for the user. Alternately, you can measure the flow rate and if it is less than 0.1 litre/minute, then the "swirl & dump "maintenance is required.

Steps:
1. Remove the filter lid.
2. If there is no water above the diffuser, add about 4 litres (1 gallon) of water.
3. Remove the diffuser.
4. Using the palm of your hand, lightly touch the very top of the sand and move your hand in a circular motion; be careful to not mix the top of the sand deeper into the filter.
5. Scoop out the dirty water with a small container.

6. Dump the dirty water outside the house in soak pit or garden.
7. Make certain the sand is smooth and level.
8. Replace the diffuser.
9. Wash your hands with soap and water.
10. Set up the storage container to collect the filtered water.
11. Refill the filter.
12. Repeat the swirl & dump steps until the flow rate has been restored.

The biolayer has been disturbed by the swirl and dump, but it will develop again over time. It is recommended to disinfect the filtered water during this time.

Notes

(Apologies for any weblinks that have been altered since publication.)

1. Edward Goldsmith, "Deindustrializing Society," The Ecologist Vol. 7. No. 4, May 1977, viewed on *Resurgence.org* archives, https://www.resurgence.org/grafix/ecologist/covers/600/1977-05.jpg.
2. J.R.R. Tolkien, *Lord of the Rings* (Boston: Houghton-Mifflin,1994), 319.
3. https://folkschoolalliance.org/a-brief-history-of-folk-schools/.
4. Rumi, "That Lives in Us," translated by Daniel Ladinsky, *Love Poems from God: Twelve Sacred Voices from the East and West*, on *Poet Seers*, https://www.poetseers.org/the-poetseers/rumi/1-2-2/).
5. Teresa, Saint, of Avila, *The Way of Perfection*, Prologue, trans. E. Allison Peers, https://cat.xula.edu/tpr/works/perfection/.
6. The Gospel of Thomas, Logion 2, trans. Lynn Bauman, quoted in Kimberly Beyer-Nelson, *Yeshua's Yoga: The Non-Dual Consciousness Teachings of the Gospel of Thomas* (2014) 38.
7. Tolkien, 901.
8. Wendell Berry, *The Need to Be Whole: Patriotism and the History of Prejudice* (Berkeley: Shoemake & Company, 2022) 29.
9. The ideals called "eternal verities" may be capitalized or not. Because I use the words often and in different ways, I choose not to capitalize.
10. Cynthia Bourgeault, "More than a body: the subtle art of cosmic reciprocity with Cynthia Bourgeault," *SPARK*, https://sparkcoaching.ca/subtle-art-of-cosmic-reciprocity-with-cynthia-bourgeault/.
11. Berry, *The Great Work* (New York: Bell Tower, 1999) 13.
12. Aldo Leopold, *A Sand County Almanac* (New York: Ballantine, 1970) 262.
13. Bourgeault, "More than a body."
14. Rumi, "That Lives in Us."
15. Thich Nhat Hanh, *Mindfulness Bell*, #14 Autumn 1995.
16. Tolkien, 231-232.
17. Teresa of Avila, *The Way of Perfection*, in Daniel Ladinsky, "Love Poems from God," *Spirituality and Practice*, https://www.spiritualityandpractice.com/book-reviews/view/5158/love-poems-from-god.
18. Thich Nhat Hanh, *Mindfulness Bell*, #14 Autumn 1995.
19. Alfred North Whitehead, *Process and Reality*, corrected edition by David Ray Griffin and Donald W. Sherburne (New York: Macmillan Publishing Co., Inc., 1978) 7.
20. David Bentley Hart, *The Experience of God* (New Haven: Yale University Press, 2013) 45.
21. Matthew 14:27-31 KJV.
22. Andreas Weber, *The Biology of Wonder* (Canada: New Society Publishers, 2016) 154-155.
23. Berry, *The Dream of the Earth*, 112-113.
24. Morris Berman, *Coming To Our Senses: Body and Spirit in the Hidden History of the West* (London: Unwin, 1989) 139.

25 David Bohm Quotes, *Wholeness and the Implicate Order* 1980, https://en.wikiquote.org/wiki/David_Bohm.
26 Bourgeault, "More than a body."
27 Edward E. Baptist in an interview by P.R. Lockhart on *Vox* Aug 16, 2019, https://www.vox.com/identities/2019/8/16/20806069/slavery-economy-capitalism-violence-cotton-edward-baptist.
28 Tolkien, 912, 917.
29 Rumi, "That Lives in Us."
30 Hanh, *Mindfulness Bell*, #14 Autumn 1995.
31 Alice Miller, "The Essential Role of an Enlightened Witness in Society," 1997, https://www.alice-miller.com/en/the-essential-role-of-an-enlightened-witness-in-society/.
32 Lyrics by The Plastic People of the Universe, quoted by John Hartzog, "Rock n' Roll: Vaclav Havel and the Birth of Charter 77," March 17, 2007, https://hartzog.org/j/havelppu2.html.
33 Vaclav Havel, "The Power of the Powerless," October 1978, https://web.archive.org/web/20120107141633/http://www.vaclavhavel.cz/showtrans.php?cat=clanky&val=72_aj_clanky.html&typ=HTML.
34 Havel, "The Power of the Powerless."
35 Jeremy Lent, *The Web of Meaning* (Canada: New Society Publishers, 2021) 388.
36 Quoted in Rutger Bregman, *Humankind: A Hopeful History* (Little, Brown and Company: New York, 2019) 253-4.
37 Rumi, "That Lives in Us."
38 William Stafford, "The Way It Is," *Ask Me: 100 Essential Poems* quoted on *Gratefulness*, https://gratefulness.org/resource/the-way-it-is-william-stafford/.
39 Etty Hillesum, *Etty: A Diary 1941-1943*, in Rosenberg, *Non-Violent Communication:A Language of Life*, p. 2.
40 https://humanorigins.si.edu/evidence/human-fossils/species/homo-sapiens.
41 Brian Hare, Vanessa Woods, *Survival of the Friendliest: Understanding Our Origins and Rediscovering Our Common Humanity* (New York: Random House, 2020), sample pages on https://www.amazon.com/Survival-Friendliest-Understanding-Rediscovering-Humanity/dp/0399590684/?asin=0399590684&revisionId=&format=4&depth=1.
42 Christopher Boehm, *Moral Origins: The Evolution of Virtue, Altruism, and Shame* (New York: Basic Books, 2012), 7.
43 Boehm, *Moral Origins*, 135.
44 Jane Elliot's famous classroom experiment to show the harm of villainizing human characteristics, see https://www.azcentral.com/story/news/local/karinabland/2017/11/17/blue-eyes-brown-eyes-jane-elliotts-exercise-race-50-years-later/860287001/.
45 Cited in Rutger Bregman, *Humankind: A Hopeful History* (Little, Brown and Company: New York, 2019), 361.
46 Joshua Barajas, "How the Nazi's defense of 'just following orders' plays out in the mind," *Science*, Feb 20, 2016, https://www.pbs.org/newshour/science/how-the-nazis-defense-of-just-following-orders-plays-out-in-the-mind.

47 There have always been a few people in every population, usually males, who could be classified as psychopathic—which most experts see as a condition from birth. Sociopaths may behave in similar ways but are more likely to have been shaped that way after birth. https://www.verywellmind.com/what-is-a-sociopath-380184.
48 Doron Shultziner et al, "The causes and scope of political egalitarianism during the last glacial: a multi-disciplinary perspective," Political Egalitarianism Project (PEP), *Springer Science+Business Media*, https://sites.lsa.umich.edu/wp-content/uploads/sites/62/2014/03/Schultziner_etal_2010_Biol_Philos.pdf.
49 Richard B. Lee, *The Dobe Ju/'hoansi*, quoted in Gray, 491.
50 Tyson Yunkaporta, *Sand Talk: How Indigenous Thinking Can Save the World* (New York: HarperCollins, 2021), 30.
51 Boehm, *Hierarchy in the Forest: The Evolution of Egalitarian Behavior* (Cambridge: Harvard University Press, 1999) 3-4.
52 James Woodburn, "Egalitarian Societies," *Limited Wants*, ed. Gowdy, 103.
53 Bruce Knaupf, quoted by Steve Taylor, "Humans aren't inherently selfish: We're actually hardwired to work together," *The Conversation*, August 21, 2020, https://phys.org/news/2020-08-humans-inherently-selfish-hardwired.html.
54 Peter Gray, "Play as a Foundation for Hunter-Gatherer Social Existence," *Journal of Play* Volume 1 #4, https://www.journalofplay.org/sites/www.journalofplay.org/files/pdf-articles/1-4-article-hunter-gatherer-social-existence.pdf.
55 Eleanor Leacock, "Women's Status in Egalitarian Society: Implications for Social Evolution," *Limited Wants, Unlimited Means: A Reader on Hunter-Gatherer Economics and the Environment*, ed. John Gowdy (Washington: Island Press, 1998) 143-145.
56 Boehm, *Moral Origins*, 330-331.
57 Boehm, *Hierarchy*, 3.
58 Yunkaporta, 27.
59 David Graeber and David Wengrow, *The Dawn of Everything: A New History of Humanity* (New York: Farrar, Strauss and Giroux), various.
60 Graeber and Wengrow, "Ancient History Shows How We Can Create a More Equal World," *NY Times*, November 4, 2021, https://www.nytimes.com/2021/11/04/opinion/graeber-wengrow-dawn-of-everything-history.html.
61 Hanh, *Call Me by My True Names: The Collected Poetry of Thich Nhat Hanh* (Berkeley, California: Parallax Press, 2001).
62 Joe Teffo, *The Concept of Ubuntu as a Cohesive Moral Value* (Pretoria: Ubuntu School of Philosophy, 1994) 12, referenced by Leonard Tumaini Chuwa, *Interpreting the Culture of Ubuntu*, https://dsc.duq.edu/cgi/viewcontent.cgi?article=1421&context=etd.
63 https://orphanwisdom.com/.
64 Robin Kimmerer, interviewed by *Citizen Potawatomi Nation*, November 3, 2015, https://www.potawatomi.org/blog/2015/11/03/q-a-with-robin-wall-kimmerer-ph-d/.

65 Berry, *Dream of the Earth*, 182, 184.
66 Martín Prechtel, *The Unlikely Peace at Cuchumaquic* (Berkeley: North Atlantic Books, 2012) 45-46.
67 Prechtel, 46.
68 Dante Alighieri, "The Love of God, Unutterable and Perfect," *Purgatorio* xv, 67-75. Virgil is speaking. Quoted in *The Enlightened Heart: An Anthology of Sacred Poetry*, edited by Stephen Mitchell (New York: HarperCollins Publishers, 1989) page 68.
69 M. Scott Peck, *The Different Drum: Community Making and Peace* (New York: Simon and Schuster, 1988) viewed at Chapter V, https://secureservercdn.net/198.71.233.111/45e.6eb.myftpupload.com/wp-content/uploads/2019/04/The-Different-Drum-Chapter-5.pdf.
70 Gray, 508.
71 Elizabeth Marshall Thomas, *The Old Way: A Story of the First People* (2006), 218, quoted in Gray, 508. Widely spaced births is a common result of a 3-4 year nursing period, or may be due to somewhat common infanticide.
72 Marshall B. Rosenberg, *Non-Violent Communication: A Language of Life* (Encinitas CA: PuddleDancer Press, 2015) 3.
73 Rosenberg, 23.
74 Roger T. Ames and David L. Hall, *Dao de Jing* "Making This Life Significant:" *A Philosophical Translation* (New York: Ballantine Books, 2003) 39.
75 Rosenberg, 64.
76 Thom Bond, *The Compassion Book: Lessons From the Compassion Course* (Orange Lake NY:One Human Publishing, 2018) 2-3.
77 Rachel Gordon, "Acceptance, Non-Attachment & Surrender: How Buddhist Principles Decrease Stress," *Humble Warrior Therapy*, November 12, 2018, https://humblewarriortherapy.com/acceptance-non-attachment-surrender-how-buddhist-principles-decrease-stress/.
78 Khushal Khan Khattak (the national poet of Afghanistan), "Know thou well this world its state," translated by C. E. Biddulph, https://poets.org/poem/know-thou-well-world-its-state.
79 Dimitri Orlov, "The Five Stages of Collapse," *Club Orlov*, February 22, 2008, https://cluborlov.blogspot.com/2008/02/five-stages-of-collapse.html.
80 Maya Angelou, "Alone," *Oh Pray My Wings Are Gonna Fit Me Well*, found on *Poets.org*, https://poets.org/poem/alone.
81 Jeremy Lent, *The Patterning Instinct: A Cultural History of Humanity's Search for Meaning* (New York: Prometheus Books, 2017) 94-5.
82 Bregman, *Humankind*, 72.
83 Bregman, *Humankind*, 22-40.
84 Martin Buber, *I and Thou*, quoted on Goodreads, https://www.goodreads.com/work/quotes/539106-ich-und-du?page=2.
85 Kimmerer, "Nature Needs a New Pronoun: To Stop the Age of Extinction, Let's Start by Ditching 'It'," *Yesmagazine*, March 30, 2015, https://www.yesmagazine.org/issue/together-earth/2015/03/30/alternative-grammar-a-new-language-of-kinship.

86 Hanh, *The Heart of Understanding*, quoted on Forum Newsletter, February 2, 2022, https://fore.yale.edu/news/Forum-Newsletter-February-2022.
87 Danusha Laméris, Small Kindnesses," first published in *Healing the Divide: Poems of Kindness and Connection* from Green Writers Press. Found on http://www.danushalameris.com/poems.html.
88 Prechtel, 47.
89 Bruno Latour, "The pandemic is a warning: we must take care of the earth, our only home," *The Guardian*, December 21, 2021, https://www.theguardian.com/commentisfree/2021/dec/24/pandemic-earth-lockdowns-climate-crisis-environment.
90 Vicki Robin, "What Could Possibly Go Right?: Episode 53," August 17, 2021, *Resilience*, https://www.resilience.org/stories/2021-08-17/what-could-possibly-go-right-episode-53/.
91 Berry, *The Dream of the Earth*, 69.
92 Abraham Lincoln, "Annual Message to Congress, Concluding Remarks," December 1, 1862, http://www.abrahamlincolnonline.org/lincoln/speeches/congress.htm.
93 Richard Heinberg, A simple way to understand what's happening ... and what to do," *Resilience*, October 20, 2020, https://www.resilience.org/stories/2020-10-20/a-simple-way-to-understand-whats-happening-and-what-to-do/.
94 Khāwje Shams-od-Din Mohammad Hāfez-e Shirizi known by his pen name Hafez or Hafiz, "Created for Joy," read on *LioninSunHeartTumblr*, January 9, 2022, https://lioninsunheart.tumblr.com/post/649357605674811392/i-sometimes-forget-that-i-was-created-for-joy-my.
95 Robert Frost, "A Time to Talk," viewed on *Poets.org*, https://poets.org/poem/time-talk.
96 Alex Steffen, "We're not yet ready for what's already happened: Welcome to discontinuity, population: everyone," *The Snap Forward*, May 18, 2021, https://alexsteffen.substack.com/p/were-not-yet-ready-for-whats-already.
97 Hannah Kuchler, "Super-rich fortify against climate change and health risks," *Financial Times*, November 13, 2020, https://www.ft.com/content/79781c20-051d-41c4-bd2c-31ceffb763e8.
98 John B. Cobb, Jr, "Ten Ideas for Saving the Planet," *Open Horizons*, https://www.openhorizons.org/ten-ideas-for-saving-the-planet.html.
99 Aleksandr I. Solzhenitsyn, The Gulag Archipelago 1918–1956, quoted on Goodreads, https://www.goodreads.com/work/quotes/2944012-arhipelag-gulag-1918-1956.
100 Shelby Stanger, "Transcript: The Power of Choice with Dr. Edith Eger," *rei.com*, May 20, 2019, https://www.rei.com/blog/podcasts/transcript-the-power-of-choice-with-dr-edith-eger.
101 Mark Boyle, *The Way Home: Tales from a life without Technology* (London: Oneworld Publications, 2019),12, 150, 210-211, 213, 215, 223, 243-44, 245-6.
102 John Michael Greer, *Green Wizardry* (Gabriola Island BC Canada: New Society Publishers, 2013) viii.

103 Carol Hupping Stoner, ed, *Producing Your Own Power* (New York: Random House, 1975).
104 https://en.wikipedia.org/wiki/Amish.
105 "Resilience-Based Organizing," Movement Generation Justice and Ecology Project, https://movementgeneration.org/resources/key-concepts/resiliencebasedorganizing/.
106 Henry A. Giroux, "The US Is Descending Into a Crisis of Overt Fascism. There's Still a Way Out," Truthout, July 14, 2022, https://truthout.org/articles/the-us-is-descending-into-a-crisis-of-overt-fascism-theres-still-a-way-out.
107 David Holmgren, "The Apology: From Baby Boomers to the Handicapped Generations," *Resilience*, March 19, 2019 (originally published in 2018 by Holmgren Design blog), https://www.resilience.org/stories/2019-03-19/the-apology-from-baby-boomers-to-the-handicapped-generations/.
108 Dmitry Orlov, *Reinventing Collapse: The Soviet Experience and American Prospects* (Gabriola Island BC Canada: New Society Publishers, 2011) 90.
109 Matthew Crawford, *Shop Class as Soulcaft: An Inquiry into the Value of Work* (New York: Penguin Press, 2009) 69.
110 Greer, *The Long Descent* (Gabriola Island BC Canada: New Society Publishers, 2008) 195.
111 Chauncey Devega, "As billionaires prep for the apocalyptic 'Event,' what happens to everyone else?," *Salon*, September 2, 2019, https://www.salon.com/2019/09/02/surviving-an-apocalypse-of-greed-as-billionaires-prep-for-the-event-what-about-the-rest-of-us/.
112 Angela Morgan, "Work: A Song of Triumph," published by *East-West Magazine* and republished at http://www.mysticalportal.net/index1.html.
113 Scott Wilson, "As it enters a third year, California's drought is strangling the farming industry," *Washington Post*, March 21, 2022, https://www.washingtonpost.com/nation/2022/03/21/california-drought-vanishing-farms.
114 Bill Weir, "Thousands of acres are underwater in California, and the flood could triple in size this summer," *CNN*, April 15, 2023, https://www.cnn.com/2023/04/15/us/tulare-lake-california-flood-climate/index.html.
115 Steve Solomon, *Gardening When It Counts: Growing Food in Hard Times* (Gabriola Island BC Canada: New Society Publishers, 2005) 21.
116 https://en.wikipedia.org/wiki/Morrill_Land-Grant_Acts.
117 Somini Sengupta, *New York Times Climate Forward*, April 29, 2022, https://www.nytimes.com/2022/04/29/climate/drought-water-scarcity.html.
118 Brad Plumer quoting author David Sedlak (Water 4.0: The Past, Present, and Future of the World's Most Vital Resource), "Our cities' water systems are becoming obsolete. What will replace them?," *Vox*, December 19, 2014, https://www.vox.com/2014/10/6/6900959/water-systems-pollution-drinking-water-desalination.
119 Earth's hydrologic cycle: (1) Surface water evaporates by energy of the sun. (2) The water vapor then forms clouds in the sky. (3) Depending on the temperature and weather conditions, the water vapor condenses and falls to the earth as rain, snow, sleet, or hail. (4) This precipitation moves

NOTES

from high areas to low areas on the earth's surface and eventually into the ground. Eventually, after years of underground movement, the groundwater comes to a discharge area where it enters a lake or stream and becomes surface water. There, the water will once again be evaporated and begin the cycle again.

120 Groundwater Foundation.
121 Aric McBay, *Peak Oil Survival* (Guilford CT: The Lyons Press, 2006) 4-7.
122 NSF/ANSI 61 is the legally recognized national standard in the United States for the human health effects assessment of drinking water contact materials, components and devices.
123 Table is based on information from the US Centers for Disease Control and Prevention, https://www.cdc.gov/healthywater/drinking/home-water-treatment/household_water_treatment.html.
124 https://sswm.info/sswm-solutions-bop-markets/affordable-wash-services-and-products/affordable-water-supply/biosand-filter.
125 https://sswm.info/sites/default/files/reference_attachments/CAWST%202009%20Biosand%20Filter%20Manual.pdf.
126 Logan Parker, "Biological Sand House Filter," https://www.youtube.com/watch?v=L56q_pCxULc. Design plans are available from Heirloom Builders, Chapel Hill NC, https://www.heirloombuilders.com/designs-for-sale/rainwater.
127 Red Flint Sand and Gravel, https://www.redflint.com/sand-filtration-media/.
128 http://www.greenstar.org/UVWaterworks.htm.
129 "Rainwater Cisterns: Design, Construction, and Treatment," June 2, 2016, https://extension.psu.edu/rainwater-cisterns-design-construction-and-treatment.
130 https://www.pendercountync.gov/utl/water-conservation-tips/.
131 Viveka Neveln, "How to Make a Rain Barrel from a Garbage Can in 5 Easy Steps," *Better Homes and Gardens*, March 3, 2022, https://www.bhg.com/gardening/design/projects/how-to-make-rain-barrel/. (1) Drill a hole slightly smaller than the diameter of the spigot four or five inches from the bottom. (2) Place a metal washer onto the threaded end of the spigot, then put a snugly fitting rubber washer over the threads to help hold the washer in place and prevent leakage. (3) Apply waterproof sealant over your rubber washer and insert the spigot into the hole on the outside wall of your barrel. (4) Allow the sealant to dry, then run a rubber washer, followed by a metal washer onto the threads of the spigot inside the barrel. (5) Secure the spigot in place inside your barrel with a nut.(6) Carefully cut a hole in the lid of your rain barrel. This hole should sit under the downspout so the water runs down into the barrel. (7) Cut the hole so it's large enough to accommodate the water flow from the downspout. (8) Drill an overflow hole near the top of your rain barrel. You can run a short length of hose or PVC pipe from the overflow hole to another rain barrel to connect them. Then, if your first rain barrel fills up, the excess water will run into the next one and you won't lose overflow water.(9) Cut a piece of landscaping fabric or screen to sit over the top, with at least a couple of inches hanging over

the side. Then, put the lid over the top of it to secure it in place, trimming away excess screen or fabric. This will keep debris from your roof out of your water and prevent mosquitoes from getting into your rain barrel.(10) With a hacksaw, cut the downspout just above the height of the barrel opening. Position the barrel directly under the downspout. It's best to raise the height of the rain barrel, setting it on a sturdy platform such as a low stack of bricks or cinder blocks. This will help gravity push water out, and with enough elevation, you may be able to fill up watering cans directly from the spigot.

132 https://www.youtube.com/watch?v=yuWdIzG9cf4.
133 https://www.almanac.com/what-hugelkultur-ultimate-raised-bed.
134 https://www.permaculture.co.uk/articles/many-benefits-hugelkultur.
135 http://crkeyline.ca/what-is-keyline-design/.
136 P.A. Yeomans, *Water for Every Farm: Yeomans Keyline Plan* (South Australia: Griffin Press Ltd., 1993).
137 http://yeomansplow.com.au/6-the-subsoil-plow-story/#top.
138 https://www.scientificamerican.com/article/skies-are-sucking-more-water-from-the-land/.
139 US Geological Survey, Estimated Use of Water in the United States, 2015, https://www.epa.gov/watersense/statistics-and-facts.
140 https://www.pendercountync.gov/utl/water-conservation-tips/.
141 https://drizzleanddip.com/2018/02/05/grilled-soy-and-lime-hake-with-charred-greens-fresh-tomato-a-chili-dressing-ways-to-save-water-in-the-kitchen/.
142 https://www.usgs.gov/special-topics/water-science-school/science/thermoelectric-power-water-use.
143 https://www.epa.gov/sustainability/lean-water-toolkit-chapter-2.
144 https://www.un.org/waterforlifedecade/pdf/human_right_to_water_and_sanitation_media_brief.pdf.
145 https://www.unicef.org/wash/water-scarcity.
146 Lisa Sorg, "Another sewage and water crisis in Currituck County," *The Pulse*, November 22, 2021, https://pulse.ncpolicywatch.org/2021/11/22/another-sewage-and-water-crisis-in-currituck-county.
147 Kavya Balaraman, "Sewage Floods Likely to Rise," *Scientific American*, August 19, 2016, https://www.scientificamerican.com/article/sewage-floods-likely-to-rise/.
148 Septic tank information from https://www.epa.gov/septic/types-septic-systems#septictank, also https://extension.unh.edu/blog/2019/12/it-okay-plant-garden-over-leach-field.
149 Brian Barth, "Humanure: The Next Frontier in Composting," *Modern Farmer*, March 7, 2017, https://modernfarmer.com/2017/03/humanure-next-frontier-composting/.
150 Joseph C. Jenkins, *The Humanure Handbook*, Fourth edition (Grove City PA: Joseph Jenkins, 2019) 216.
151 Jenkins, 216-217, 223.

152 Jenkins, 218.
153 Jenkins, 225.
154 Jenkins, 235.
155 Jenkins, 225-227.
156 Jenkins, 240-241.
157 Jenkins, 229.
158 Jenkins, 236.
159 Jenkins, 79, 90.
160 Jenkins, 83.
161 Jenkins, 126.
162 Jenkins, 128-132.
163 Jenkins, 249.
164 Jenkins, 248.
165 Jenkins, 155-156.
166 Jenkins, 291, quoting Feachem et al, *Appropriate Technology for Water Supply and Sanitation* (Washington DC: The World Bank, Director of Information and Public Affairs, 1980).
167 Jenkins, 196.
168 Jenkins, 234.
169 Jenkins, 170.
170 David the Good, *Compost Everything: The Good Guide to Extreme Composting*, (FL: Good Books Publishing, 2021) 73, 79-80.
171 David the Good, 65-66.
172 https://en.wikipedia.org/wiki/Ideonella_sakaiensis.
173 https://en.wikipedia.org/wiki/Zophobas_morio.
174 Damion Carrington, "Wax worm saliva rapidly breaks down plastic bags, scientists discover," *The Guardian*, October 4, 2022, https://www.theguardian.com/environment/2022/oct/04/wax-worm-saliva-rapidly-breaks-down-plastic-bags-scientists-discover.
175 https://www.science.org/content/article/could-plastic-eating-microbes-take-bite-out-recycling-problem.
176 Tim Dickinson, "How Big Oil and Big Soda kept a global environmental calamity a secret for decades," *Rolling Stone*, March 3, 2020, https://www.rollingstone.com/culture/culture-features/plastic-problem-recycling-myth-big-oil-950957; "The toxic killers in our air too small to see," BBC Future, November 15, 2019, https://www.bbc.com/future/article/20191113-the-toxic-killers-in-our-air-too-small-to-see.
177 Orlov, *Reinventing Collapse*, 150.
178 Stephen Harrod Buhner, *The Lost Language of Plants* (White River Junction VT: Chelsea Green, 2002) 120.
179 Rodney Merrill, "Remove toxics from your home by switching to 'natural' household cleaners," *Backwoods Home Magazine*, February 1991 Issue #7, now unavailable; quoted in Carla Emery, *The Encyclopedia of Country Living* (Seattle: Sasquatch Books, 2012) 70.

180 https://www.gardeningknowhow.com/edible/herbs/soapwort/soapwort-plant.htm.
181 Brooks Eliot Wigginton, *The Foxfire Book* (Garden City NY: Anchor Books, 1972).
182 https://jlmissouri.com/wp-content/uploads/2013/03/Foxfire-1.pdf.
183 https://www.britannica.com/plant/horsetail; https://partridgepineandpeavey.wordpress.com/2016/02/16/horsetail-or-scouring-rush/.
184 https://www.grandpappy.org/hsksoap.htm.
185 https://farmingmybackyard.com/homemade-soap-from-ashes/.
186 Kristopher Drummond, "Regenesis," *Kristopher Drummond Blog*, September 7, 2020, https://www.kristopherdrummond.com/post/regenesis.
187 Margaret J. Wheatley, Warriors for the Human Spirit, https://margaretwheatley.com/.
188 Often attributed to martyred Bishop Oscar Romero, this prayer was composed by Bishop Ken Untener in November 1979. https://www.bread.org/article/a-prayer-of-oscar-romero/#:~:text=We%20are%20prophets%20of%20a,that%20they%20hold%20future%20promise.
189 Fred LaMotte, "Ancestry," *A New Republic of the Heart*, June 24, 2021, https://newrepublicoftheheart.org/podcast/073-fred-lamotte-from-the-temple-to-the-wilderness-of-now/.
190 J. Allen Boone, *Kinship with All Life* (San Francisco: Harper, 1954) 7-8.
191 Stephen R. Covey, *The 7 Habits of Highly Effective People* (New York: Free Press, 1990).
192 Tolkien, 913.
193 Michael Meade, "The Path of Conscious Descent," June 9, 2024, https://mailchi.mp/carolynbaker.net/the-sun-day-post-june-9-2024.
194 Kristopher Drummond, "Regenesis."
195 Rupert Sheldrake, *A New Science of Life* (New York: J.P. Tarcher, 1981).
196 Robert Wolff, *Original Wisdom* (Rochester VT: Inner Traditions International, 2001) 157.
197 David Abram, *The Spell of the Sensuous* (New York: First Vintage Book Edition, 1997) 66.
198 Buhner, 172.
199 Berry, *Dream of the Earth*.
200 https://ecoss.org/the-universe-is-a-communion-of-subjects-not-a-collection-of-objects-thomas-berry/.
201 Frances Hodgson Burnett, *The Secret Garden* (New York: Frederick A. Stokes Company,1911). It was first published in ten issues (November 1910 – August 1911) of *The American Magazine*, with illustrations by J. Scott Williams.
202 Jane Austen, *Pride and Prejudice* (London: Thomas Egerton, 1813).
203 Post Carbon Institute, "Welcome to the Great Unraveling," June 15, 2023, https://www.postcarbon.org/publications/welcome-to-the-great-unraveling/.

Index

A

A New Science of Life 161
Abram, David 25, 163
aggression 54, 57
Alighieri, Dante 64
altruism 49, 52, 56, 74, 78
American Indian: Anishinaabe pronouns 75; history of harm 34, 61; Mayan 61–63, 79–80; Navajo 21
Ames, Roger T. 67
Amish 90–92
Angelou, Maya 71
antibiotics 149–150
Austen, Jane 165

B

bacteria 121, 122, 123, 125, 137, 138, 139, 140, 143, 144, 148, 149
Berman, Morris 31
Berry, Thomas 16, 27, 61, 81, 164
Berry, Wendell 13
Biblical quotes (KJV) 14, 17, 18, 29, 37, 42, 43, 78
biosand filters 123–125, 175–184
blue eyes experiment 54, 186
Boehm, Christopher 54, 55, 56, 57
Bohm, David 31, 162
Bond, Thom 69
Boone, J. Allen 157–158
Bourgeault, Cynthia 14, 17, 33
Boyle, Mark 90, 91
boys 74, 76
Bregman, Rutger 72, 73
Buber, Martin 75
Buddhist Joanna Macy 12
Buddhist non-attachment 69
Buhner, Stephen Harrod 149, 150, 163
Burnett, Frances Hodgson 164

C

California weather affecting food supply 190
childrearing 65–66
cleaning 148–151
Cobb, John B. Jr. 87
collapse 70, 87, 89
Coming to Our Senses 161
communal, communality 55-63, 74, 76
communication 53, 57, 66, 67, 70, 163
communication barriers 65, 66, 67
community 74–78
compost dangerous trash 146–147
compost simple 141
cooperation or co-operation 4, 53, 56, 58, 60, 66, 72–73, 166
Covey, Stephen J. 158
Crawford, Matthew 97

D

Dao de Jing 67, 78
David the Good 146
death 22, 43
DIY rain barrel 191
DIY water filter 122
drought 79, 111, 125, 133, 168
Drummond, Kristopher 153,160
dualism, materialism, reductionism 13, 31, 37, 41, 161, 162

E

egalitarian 28, 52, 53–58, 73
Eger, Edith 88
evil 12, 20–21, 24–25, 26, 66
extension services, state and county 115, 126, 127

F

fairness 29, 33-36
fertilizers 104, 108, 132, 138
folk schools 5
food 100–115
forgiveness 30

Foxfire books 151
Frost, Robert 82

G

gardening. *See* food
genetic traits. *See* human evolutionary nature
God 18, 23, 78
Golding, William 73
Goldsmith, Edward 1
Gordon, Rachel 69
Graeber, David 57
Grahame, Kenneth 32
Gray, Peter 65
Great Depression 95
Greer, John Michael 90, 97

H

Hafez 82
Hall, David L. 67
Hanh, Thich Nhat 21, 37, 59, 76
Hare, Brian 52
Hart, David Bentley 24
Havel, Vaclav 39, 40
Heinberg, Richard 81
Heirloom Builders 124
hierarchy 54, 57, 58,
Hillesum, Etty 52, 53, 54
Holmgren, David 96
horsetail plant 151
hugelkultur 130
human evolutionary nature 52–54
humanure 138–145
hunter-gatherer 54, 56, 65
hydrologic cycle 118

I

I'm well if you're well 58, 59, 64
Indigenous 21, 55, 59, 75, 77, 162, 163
individualism 56, 63, 75
industrialization 63, 88, 96, 153
integrity 28
intentional community 5, 66, 71, 72, 73, 167

J

Jenkins, Joseph 104
Jenkinson, Stephen 61
Ju/'hoansi 55
justice. *See* Fairness

K

Keyline design 130–132
Khattak, Khushal Khan 70
Kimmerer, Robin Wall 61, 75
kindness 28, 32
Knaupf, Bruce 54, 55
Kuchler, Hannah 87
Kunstler, James Howard 89

L

Laméris, Danusha 77
LaMotte, Fred 157
Latour, Bruno 80
Leacock, Eleanor 56
Lee, Richard B. 55
Lent, Jeremy 41, 72
Leopold, Aldo 17, 24
Lincoln, Abraham 81
loneliness 72, 158, 174
love 23, 30, 32, 37, 64, 78, 155
loyalty 28, 32

M

materialism. *See* dualism
McBay, Aric 118, 135
Meade, Michael 160
Merrill, Rodney 150
Miller, Alice 38
miracles 25
Morgan, Angela 98
Morrill Land Grant Acts. *See* extension services
Movement Generation 92

N

nanoplastics 148
nature 26, 27
Nazism 53, 54, 88

non-violent 76
nonviolent communication overview 66
nonviolent communication steps of process 67–69

O

Original Wisdom 162
Orlov, Dmitri 70–71, 96
Orphan Wisdom 61

P

Peck, M. Scott 64–65
personal agency 93, 97, 98
plastic eating microbes 148
Plastic People of the Universe 39
Post Carbon Institute 153
Prechtel, Martín 61–63, 79–80
Pride and Prejudice 165

R

reductionism. *See* dualism
religion 15, 16, 21, 27, 63
Robin, Vicki 81
Rosenberg, Marshall 67–69, 76, 78
Rumi 10, 19, 37, 43
Russell, Bertrand 41

S

sacrifice 29
self-provisioning 89, 93, 96, 98, 99
Senegal 74
septic tanks 137
sewage overflow 136, 147
Sheldrake, Rupert 161
Sheridan, Rob 98
slavery 34, 53
soapwort 151
Solomon, Steve 104, 115
Solzhenitsyn, Aleksandr I 87
South Africa 59
spiritual 10, 15, 16, 17, 21, 22, 23, 25, 26, 27, 30, 31, 34, 37, 40, 42, 51, 78, 155, 162
Stafford, William 44
Steffen, Alex 87

T

Teresa, of Avila 11, 20
The Dream of the Earth 164
The Lord of the Rings 165
The Lost Language of Plants 163
The Secret Garden 164
The Spell of the Sensuous 163
Thomas, Elizabeth Marshall 66
Thomas, Gospel of 11
thou 75
Tolkien 2, 12, 19, 32, 36, 44, 159, 165
truth 30–31, 37–41

U

ubuntu 59
Untener, Ken 156

V

vegetables culture 105–116
vegetables fencing 113
vegetables insects 114
vegetables seed saving 110
vegetables storage 105
verities, eternal 14, 17, 33, 44
village-mindedness 74, 76, 78, 166, 174

W

Wallace, Henry 95
water conservation 132–134
water purification 121–125
water quality community water systems 118
water quality wells 119
water rights 119
water scarcity 117
water storage 126–130
water usage human average need 134
water usage US average usage 134
water wells 118–119
Weber, Andreas 26, 27
Wengrow, David 57
Wheatley, Meg 155
Whitehead, Alfred North 23
Wholeness and the Implicate Order 162

Wind in the Willows 32
Wolff, Robert 162
Woodburn, James 55
Woods, Vanessa 52
World War II 5, 60

Y

Yeomans, P.A. 130, 131, 135
Yunkaporta, Tyson 55, 57

Z

Zimbabwe 58
Zulu 59

Printed in the USA
CPSIA information can be obtained
at www.ICGtesting.com
LVHW051504301024
795099LV00006B/576